Twilight Visitors:

Volume One

Now read about hauntings, ghosts and
poltergeists compiled by

Sharon A. Gill
&
Dave R. Oester

as

THE
GHOST
WRITERS

as seen by millions of viewers on

ABC NEWS NIGHTLINE
ABC WORLD NEWS
&
NBC GOOD EVENING
NBC EVENING MAGAZINE

Twilight Visitors:

True Tales of Hauntings,
Ghosts & Active Unseen Visitors

Volume One

Collected and Edited by
Sharon A. Gill & Dave R. Oester

A StarWest Book

Twilight Visitors: Ghost Tales!
Volume One
Copyright © 1995 by Sharon A. Gill Living Trust

Book cover design: StarWest Images
Photographs: Sharon A. Gill
Front book cover: Neer City Cemetery, Goble, Oregon
Composition: Word Perfect For Windows 6.0a
Typesetting & Layout: PageMaker 5.0 for Windows
Photography Layout: Photoshop 2.51 for Windows

First Edition
First Printing; March 1995

ISBN: 1-885591-84-5

Additional copies are available. For your convenience, an order form can be found at the back of this book.

Published By:
StarWest Images,
Regional Book Publisher
P. O. Box 976
St. Helens, OR 97051
(503) 397-0686

Printed in the USA by

MORRIS
PUBLISHING

3212 E. Hwy 30
Kearney, NE 68847
800-650-7888

Dedicated to the
Memory and the Spirit
of
James Madison Gill
1938-1989

Free from desire,
you realize the mystery.
Caught in desire,
you see only the manifestations.

Yet mystery and manifestations
arise from the same source.
This source is called darkness.

Darkness within darkness.
The gateway to all understanding.

Tao Te Ching
Verse 1

CONTRIBUTIONS

We would like to thank the following people for their stories concerning ghosts, haunted houses and poltergeist activities. We appreciate the time they took out of their busy schedules to send their stories to us or to meet with us in person. Without their help, this book would not have been possible. We want to thank those who helped us in researching these stories.

Adams, Cheri
Adams, Helen
Adams, Rolf
Allen, Daniel
Anonymous
Baker, Susan
Barnett, Dianna
Beck, Kat
Bergen, David
Bowles, Larissa M.
Brennan, Leanne
Burdick, Joyce M.
Burgoine, Jonathan
Burhans, Jeffrey
Cavallo, Teresa
Chiknmouse
Ebert, Dean
Emmert, Russell L.
Ford, Gary S.
Gates, Julia L.
Heil, Crystal
Kelley, Leslie
Jester, Stanley Owen
Kortlever, Ruth L.
Madson, Betty
Marlow, G. Scott
Marlow, Cindy H.

McMaster, Elena
Mills, Jonathan W.
Marrone, Darrell
Oester, Carolina E.
Oester, Hazel G.
Oester, Sarah L.
Palacios, Marco A.
Palmer, Elizabeth
Pease, Shawn
Pescuma, Michael
Rogers, Donald
Rogers, Sharon D.
Shade, Robert M.
Shaffer, Sydney O.
Shields, Frank
Shields, Rosy
Simonton, Norman
Simpson, John
Starshadow, Valanti
Vetti, David

<u>RESEARCH HELPER'S</u>

Sharon D. Rogers of Seaside, OR
Donald Rogers of Seaside, OR
Leslie Kelley of Astoria, OR
Kathy Tesar of St. Helens, OR
Pat Kosharek of Forest Grove, OR

SPECIAL THANKS TO:

ABC NEWS NIGHTLINE
NBC GOOD EVENING
NBC EVENING MAGAZINE
LIBERTY THEATER
PACIFIC UNIVERSITY
ST. HELENS SENIOR HIGH SCHOOL
ST. HELENS PUBLIC LIBRARY
ROEHMS HOME FURNISHING
COLUMBIA FUNERAL HOME
THE CHRONICLE & SENTINEL-MIST
THE DAILY ASTORIAN
THE SPOTLIGHT
FANTASTIC MUSEUM
HAZEL G. OESTER
WALT & LOLA WIDMER
GREG SPENCER

TABLE OF CONTENTS

INTRODUCTION

I can still remember sitting around the flickering flames of a cedar campfire as a young Boy Scout eagerly listening to the scary stories only told to older Scouts. I listened as our devoted Scoutmaster narrated old spooky tales about ghosts, haunted houses and things that go bump in the night.

The young Boy Scouts would sit around the campfire, glued to the haunting words uttered by our Scoutmaster. Vivid images of horror and terror filled our tender and innocent minds.

One of the scariest tales I can remember from my Boy Scout camping days is unfortunately lacking actual details. It seems that over the years, I have obliterated the story from the gray cells of my adult mind. However, I can still clearly remember the title of the most fascinating horror story from my youth. The memories of dread and fear, instilled in the mind of that young Boy Scout remains very strong and deeply rooted in my memory today. It seems that the horror tale involved a hermit who was a mad man. His name was 'Liver-Eating Johnson'.

As the tale goes, this hermit was crazy, having gone berserk from constant loneliness. This crazy hermit had become a killer of little boys, especially boys who were Boy Scouts! This mad man went around ripping out the livers of little boys, quickly eating the liver as red blood slowly dripped to the ground.

At least, according to our Scoutmaster's version of the story. Supposedly, 'Liver-Eating Johnson' would first scratch on the tent sides before ripping the tent apart and attacking the poor boys inside. After the story, we would retire for the evening.

Our Scoutmaster would come along and scratch on the sides of our tents. Four young Scouts would go wild, trying to get out of their tents for fear of having their livers ripped out and eaten! It was all done in good clean fun and we understood it and loved it, but we were still scared!

Ghost stories and tales of things that go bump in the night can be traced to our founding fathers who first stepped ashore over four hundred years ago. These ghost stories are the basis for many of America's Folklore stories.

Dave Oester
St. Helens, OR

Around the time David was sitting around the camp fire with his Boy Scout Troop, my interests became captured by the exciting adventures of the great detective, Nancy Drew. Though growing up a thousand miles apart from Dave, my love for the unusual and out-of-the-ordinary was developing.

Though Dave and I had endured various tragedies and heartbreaks in our separate lives, the time had come for us to join. Our interest, needs and desires appeared as the thinking of one mind rather than two individuals. The previous years had prepared us for our meeting and for embarking on a new life together. Our common goals were to share experiences and our accumulated knowledge with others.

Moving into a house with active and unseen inhabitants, helped give us some direction. Sharing our experiences with other people who in turn openly shared their own has brought us to the realization that Ghost Stories are common in the everyday lives of ordinary people. We came to the conclusion these stories should be documented and shared. We both loved photography so we incorporated it into our stories, photographs which could give our readers an insight into the places we wrote about.

By focusing on ghosts, haunting's and poltergeist activities, we have generated tremendous interest in the subject and have met many fine folks. We were fortunate in that we found each other along the way, developing our abilities and talents enough to produce this book to share with you, the reader.

Our hope is that the stories included within these pages will thrill and chill you. If the tales should stimulate a memory of an experience you would like to share for our next book, please feel free to write your story down and mail it to the address below or send it via E-mail on Internet. We look forwarded to hearing from you concerning our book or perhaps you know of a place that is haunted and would like us to investigate.

Write to:

StarWest Images
P.O. Box 976
St. Helens, OR 97051

Internet: Starwest@ix.netcom.com
           'The Ghost Writers'

Now sit back, relax and enjoy reading about things that go bump in the night.

Sharon Gill
St. Helens, OR

IN THE BEGINNING

It was late in October of 1993 that we had decided to purchase some furniture for our living room. We were in Roehm's Home Furnishings, a local furniture store in downtown Seaside, Oregon. We were standing at the front counter looking around while waiting for the paperwork to be completed on our purchase. To our surprise, laying on the counter was the book by Mike Helm, entitled *"Oregon Ghosts & Monsters"* that we had been talking about a few days before.

We picked up the book and started to comment about how good this book was and about some of the experiences we had over the years in our haunted house. Almost immediately the owner, Susan Baker, who was behind the counter started telling us about her experience with a ghost, who smoked cigars in her home. Susan Baker told us how actual blue rings of cigar smoke could be seen by her and her parents who did not smoke! She related cups that floated in the air without support and of a child crying in the attic of their home! Then we laughed together relating our tales of ghosts and poltergeist activities.

Later, after we had departed from the furniture store and while walking to our car, we spoke about how nice it would be if there was a book out that dealt with local stories of ghosts and hauntings. The more we talked, the more we thought we could write that book. So after several months of thinking and talking about the book, we decided we would start by placing a classified ad in a local newspaper seeking true-life experiences involving ghosts, hauntings & poltergeist activities.

Shortly after our classified ad appeared in The Daily Astorian, we received a letter from one of the staff writers, Greg Spencer. He was interested in doing an interview concerning our experiences with ghosts, hauntings and poltergeist activities on the Oregon Coast. An appointment was set up for the following week. Then at the appointed time, we showed up at the meeting place, a small deli cafe on Broadway Avenue in Seaside. We thought the interview would take thirty minutes but it expanded to an hour and a half.

It appeared that in the early part of our interview, the reporter could not decide if we were real or if we were trying to pull a fast one on him. He had that typical look of disbelief and the "Are you for real" look that is often associated with individuals who step forward and reveal their ghostly experiences.

A week later the article appeared on the front page of The Daily Astorian. We were shocked since we felt that perhaps the reporter might include a small one paragraph article about us but not the long and full article about us and our ghostly experiences. The reporter had been somewhat humorous in his approach with the article and it was very amusing, especially in his description of us as 'small town hack detectives' and as 'ghostbuster wannabe's'. We had a good laugh and enjoyed the article but thought nothing more of it.

Then by late fall we began planning to move from the Coast to the Portland area where the weather wasn't so wet and the climate warmer. We finally found a home in February and completed our move to St. Helens from the coastal town of Seaside in March. It took a few months to settle in and to get back into a writing routine

Then one morning as we checked our Post Office Box, to our surprise, we had a letter from ABC NEWS Nightline in Washington, D.C. requesting us to call them. They wanted to discuss with us a show on ghosts, hauntings and poltergeist activities. Apparently, the newspaper article was picked up on the National Wire Services and was read in Washington, D.C. by ABC NEWS Nightline.

Suddenly, we were launched into national media coverage, while we were still collecting ghost tales. We postponed the meeting with ABC NEWS Nightline since we were not prepared yet for that type of interview. Sharon and I decided it was time, so we began a full time campaign collecting Oregon ghost stories from around the local area.

Five months later we were again contacted by the Associate Producer of ABC NEWS Nightline. By this time we had gathered enough interesting stories to do justice for a half hour feature story. When the filming crew arrived on Saturday, October 21, we did not know what to expect. Kathy Kennedy, Associate Producer introduced Minh Van Dang, the Senior ABC camera man and Bruce Renwick, ABC sound man.

Once equipment had been arranged according to the direction of Minh Van Dang which would provide the best camera view, the interview with us conducted by Kathy Kennedy began and continued for over six hours. We were exhausted by the end of the first day and not so afraid of being on the other side of the video camera.

The next day, we scheduled ABC to shoot our former haunted house in Seaside and the old opera house, now the Liberty Theater in Astoria, which is haunted by none other than three ghosts. The last day of the filming involved shooting the local high school auditorium. This auditorium has been reported as being haunted with a poltergeist.

ABC NEWS Nightline aired the 30 minute program entiIted 'Ghost Writers' on November 21, 1994. The story was picked up again by ABC World News and aired early the next morning. It was estimated that over ten million people viewed the story.

Kathy Kennedy and Minh Van Dang

We were contacted by NBC Good Evening about doing a video segment on us as ghost writers. We met the crew of NBC Good Evening at the Liberty Theater and had a good time filming the story about the three ghosts who haunt that theater. NBC Good Evening aired our story in Portland and then NBC Evening Magazine in Seattle aired the story a few days later. The Liberty Theater segment has been aired several times since.

This book is the result of countless interviews with those kind people who were brave enough to relate their tales. Without their help and the help of other researchers, these stories could not be written.

The photographs will hopefully give you, the reader, a better idea of where these events took place. Some of the photographs will show what we believe to be actual apparitions' that have been photographed at various haunts.

As the authors, we believe in the merits of good, clean, old fashion folklore tales, especially those of haunted houses and ghostly apparitions and things that go bump in the night. Our purpose is not to question religious tenants or label ghosts or apparitions as being good or evil but rather to present the tales in the light of common folklore.

Dave R. Oester
Sharon A. Gill
St. Helens, 1995

OUR SEASIDE HOUSE

Seaside was established as a resort town on the coast where the people of Portland could go and get away from the summer heat, enjoying the beautiful coastal setting with its cooler temperatures. An eight thousand foot promenade borders the beach and the many homes crammed side by side, facing the beautiful Pacific ocean. Many homes were built as summer homes where families could go during the summer months at the turn of the century.

The population of Seaside climbs to over twenty-five thousand people during the summer months, returning to its normal five thousand population during the winter months. Many homes are vacant during the winter months, with occasional weekend visits by their owners. The winter months are peaceful and quiet in Seaside. The downtown business life stops at five o'clock and the streets become dead with no activity in the evenings. Local residences appreciate the quiet small town environment, free from the fast pace and traffic jams of big cities.

Our old wooden one-story house was at the foot of the 12th Avenue Bridge overlooking the Necanicum river. Our home, built in 1938, had a full basement which was consistent with the homes built back in that era. Unlike other basements, ours had a variety of ghosts and poltergeist activities.

Our spirit visitors were for the most part just mischievous entities having a good time at our expense. We often joked that we should charge rent to our spirit visitors if they were to share the house with us. There were constant poltergeist activities in the basement, which we used as storage space.

During the two years that we lived in the house, strange noises were constantly heard emulating from the basement. Often, we would be awakened hearing sounds and movement downstairs in the middle of the night. Yet never did we ever see any of the commotion take place. Sometimes it would sound like boxes falling over yet when we investigated, no boxes had fallen!

My hobby is electronics and I had a workbench set up in a corner of the basement. My workbench, filled with various tools such as soldering guns, solder, wire and a fully stocked inventory of electronic components arranged in plastic bins for constructing electronic circuits. The spirit visitors never disturbed my work bench or tools with one exception.

Electronic work bench in basement

The spirit visitors however, did have a field day with Sharon's tools she used for her arts and craft projects. Once they hung the wood burning tool from the clothes line in the basement. The wood burning tool had previously been laying on the workbench she used for her projects. However, most of the time the spirit visitors would simply 'borrow' stuff from her never returning it. Sharon is still missing two important photography books that our visitors saw fit to 'borrow' but alas so far have failed to return to their rightful owner!

DAVE OESTER'S GHOST

I am not as sensitive to the psychic vibrations emulating from our basement visitors as Sharon has been. However, I did have five experiences that took place in our home in Seaside during the two years that we lived in that house. I would like to share them with you.

THE CIRCUIT GHOST

As an Amateur Radio Operator, WA7CPI, and being electronic oriented, I would construct electronic projects dealing with square wave pulse generators operating at extremely low frequencies. I would sit at the workbench in our basement and declare that if spirit entities disturbed any of my projects, I would build an electronic ghostbusting unit that would drive the spirit entities from the house.

Apparently the spirit entities believed me for they didn't disturb any of my tools or circuits except once. The paranormal pranksters rearranged a custom-built four-layer hand-wound coil. I made this coil by wrapping multiple layers of wire around a small diameter wooden dowel.

Each layer of wire taped down with black electrical tape for insulation, then a new layer of wire wrapped over the black electrical tape. This process of winding wire over a layer of tape was repeated four times.

The ends of the coil wire were then soldered to the circuit board and placed inside a plastic construction box and sealed shut with screws. The plastic construction box can't be opened without using a very small screwdriver to remove the tiny screws which are held tightly in place.

To my amazement our basement ghost somehow reconstructed that hand-wound coil. All of the black electrical tape was below the wire and on top of the dowel. The wire was then wrapped over the top of the top layer of the black electrical tape in a helter skelter fashion. The circuit board still had the soldered coil wire ends attached. All this while the hand-wrapped coil was inside a sealed construction box held tightly closed by four screws.

It is physically impossible for this prank to have happened for several reasons. The first is that the ends of the wires were still soldered to the circuit board. Second, the black electrical tape was neatly rewound around the dowel, with the wire layers on top of the tape. There is no way this could have been done without unsoldering at least one wire from the circuit board.

The ghostly coil

THE BASEMENT VOICE

In July, 1992 three of my five children were visiting us for a few weeks. Since our home was small with only one-bedroom, we prepared separate sleeping areas in the basement for each of them. Each separated area had a cot with a sleeping bag.

The basement was quiet and cooler during the summer then the main floor of the home. Often, the children would go down to the basement during the heat of the day, curl up on their cot with a good book and enjoy a few hours of uninterrupted reading.

I was doing something upstairs when I decided I was going to ask Sarah a question. I thought she would be downstairs in the basement since I hadn't seen her for some time. I walked to the basement door and yelled down the stairs into the basement, "Sarah are you down there?"

A girl's voice responded back and said, "Yes I am down here." I decided that my question could wait as I did not want to disrupt her train of thought. I would wait until she took a reading break to ask my question.

Then I walked back through the kitchen, to the computer room where my other two children were playing games on the computer. To my surprise Sarah was playing on the computer and the other two children were watching her. I asked her how long she had been in the computer room, she responded for about an hour.

There was no way she could have gotten up from the basement and into the computer room. There is only one exit from the basement and I was standing at that exit. I had immediately walked back to the computer room. This was the first time I'd heard a "voice" from our unseen basement inhabitants!

THE MISSING FURNACE FILTER

Our home in Seaside was heated by an oil furnace and required the two paper air filters' changed regularly. The previous day, I had replaced the two old and dirty filters with two brand new filters.

The next day, I was walking downstairs to the basement to work at the electronic workbench when I noticed that one of the two filters was missing from the filter holder. I wondered at the time, how could the air filter be missing since it had to be pushed into place with some difficulty?

I went down to the local hardware store and purchased a replacement filter for the oil furnace. I returned home, walked downstairs to replace the missing filter when I discovered the missing filter returned and was positioned above the filter holder.

The missing filter was placed next to the furnace as if it was ready to be installed. I was shocked! There is no way that air filter could have been there before my departure to the store to purchase a new air filter.

There is no doubt in my mind, I know I had installed both air filters as I had difficulty inserting both filters into the filter holder. It normally takes a single filter that is very expensive and much wider. I had decided using two less expensive filters and changing them more often was more economical. I had to force the two filters into the tight fit of the filter holder.

The air filters were definitely snug in the filter holder and could not slide out on their own. Now what would a ghost need with an air filter?

WALTZING MATILDA

It was Christmas day and the U-Haul truck was finally unloaded! We had completed a twenty-two-hour drive to arrive at our new home in Seaside after loading the truck for four days straight. Now, we had three days to unload and return the truck to meet the deadline.

Unloading the truck took three long days. Boxes were stacked upon boxes, through out the house and basement. We were exhausted from the move and began slowing unpacking the boxes. All of the rooms had boxes stacked, floor to ceiling with only a walkway between the boxes to access each room.

Unpacking, we had found the shortwave radio so we had set it up in the den but we never plugged the radio into the outlet. We were busy unpacking the kitchen boxes so we could have glasses and plates for our meals. It was getting late and we had decided to stop for the day. We had sleeping bags that we were using until the bedroom could be set up.

The midnight hour came and suddenly we could hear the tune, Waltzing with Matilda, playing. The tune kept playing repeatedly, with no intermission or break. Curious, we investigated the source of the music coming from the den. We had not turned on any radio or CD players. We walked to the den and discovered that the tune was coming from the shortwave radio. We checked the radio but it was still unplugged from the electrical outlet.

After repeating itself thirteen times, the music stopped as suddenly as it had started. Exhausted from the move, we dismissed the occurence from our minds and fell asleep.

TOILET PAPER ROLL

We had been away from our home in Seaside for about a week on business. We arrived home late in the evening, unpacked the motorhome and started to settle down to unwind. I went into the bathroom and found everything as it should have been. Ten or fifteen minutes later, Sharon walked into the bathroom to find a new roll of toilet tissue, in a pile in the middle of the floor. The window was closed so no air currents could have started the roll of toilet paper to unwind. The entire roll had unwound into a big heap on the bathroom floor as a welcome home message to us. At least, that is what we suspected.

Authors Note:

These experiences have convinced the authors that there are ghosts, or perhaps we should say spirit entities that were living in the Seaside house. This author was much more skeptical then Sharon and perhaps for that reason, this author has experienced the unexplainable events described in the first five stories. It was because of these events, that our lives changed when we started writing this book on ghost stories.

SHARON GILL'S GHOSTS

MISSING PHOTO BOOKS

We had a full basement in our home in Seaside, Oregon with great bookshelves lining one side of the basement wall. I had decided that this would be an excellent spot to house all of my photography books for easy access.

I unpacked all of my photography boxes that were filled with photography books collected over the years. Some of these books were from classes I had taken at Weber State University along with many other books purchased on specific aspects of photography.

I had books on cameras', darkroom developing, filters and lenses. I had some hard to find books that I used as references that are now out of print. Several books were on outdoor shooting and nature photography since I specialized in that type of photography.

A question came up concerning photographing eagles so I went downstairs to the basement to get my books dealing with wildlife and birds. I wanted to check on what type of zoom lenses worked best for capturing wildlife on film. I went over to the bookshelf and starting thumbing my way through books looking for my university textbook that had a section on lenses for wildlife. After scanning the books on the shelf, I could not find that book or the other book specifically dealing with birds. I know I had unpacked them as I remember glancing through the books prior to placing them on the shelf. I used these books frequently for reference.

Basement book shelves

No one had borrowed those books since I refuse to loan any of my photo books out. I looked and looked and still could not find the two books. I even went so far as to stand in the basement and ask the ghosts for the books back, all to no avail.

Why the house ghosts decided to single me out I may never know, but one thing is sure, my books have never been returned to me. We lived in that house for two years. Every time I return to visit with the current tenants, I ask if my books have been returned. They are still missing and I have doubts they'll ever be returned.

DEATH OF A FRIEND

My experience took place in Laguna Beach, California and happened in April 1969 as plans for my wedding on May Second were in full swing. The colors had been chosen, patterns and material for the bridesmaids dresses had been purchased.

I was full of excitement and apprehension. I was entering a new phase of my adult life as a prospective new bride. The elation filling my being like a dense fog and all was well within my world.

My bridesmaids were all my very best of friends and my two sisters. My dearest friend, though we had actually only known each other about a year, was Liz. We had met at the hospital where we worked very closely as a team in the Emergency Room.

Liz was four years older, which made her twenty-two years old at the time. She was a petite, bright and cheery young RN, one of the best I ever had the pleasure of working with. We became the closest of friends quickly, sharing many common interests.

I loved her like a sister and respected her as the professional nurse she was. I learned a great deal from Liz, watching her perform her nursing duties in emergency conditions with ease and grace.

We talked about the wedding at length, it was only three weeks away. She had only just become engaged to the cutest young doctor in the hospital. We found ourselves dreaming the dreams of young brides, whose lives are full of love, children, homes with Victorian decor, endless futures of total bliss.

Not for one moment did a negative thought enter the pictures we painted in our minds, of the days that lie ahead of us. We knew, we always would remain the best of friends, no matter where we were, no matter how many miles came between us.

As I lay sleeping one night, I was suddenly awakened from what seemed to be a horrible dream. It was one of those nightmares, that once awake, I sat up, tears flowing down my face, wondering if it were truly a dream. Something inside my mind kept telling me that it was real. If that were the case, then my best friend, Liz, was dead! After fitfully sleeping the next few hours before dawn, I awoke still feeling strongly Liz was dead. I readied myself for work in a normal fashion, but feeling as though I was grieving.

The morning hours were relatively quiet in the Emergency Room. It was Liz's day off so I had no reason to expect to see her there. After tending to a few routine non-urgent patients, I stepped out into the hall.

I saw the head ER physician coming toward me. He was an elderly man, butch haircut and gold-rimmed glasses, not necessarily known for having a mild temperament or a compassionate manner. But as he spoke to me, his voice was soft and solemn.

"Sharon, I have some bad news for you this morning. Liz was in an automobile accident last night and was killed instantly."

I looked at his face and said, "I know." Liz and her fiance were killed in San Diego. The newspapers in our area did not carry the story of the crash. The tragic accident was not carried on the radio or television stations. For some reason, I'm sure Liz felt she must let me know she was gone.

THE HOUSE OF NO RETURN

The place had a history of affliction and tragedy associated with it. The locale was said to be the site of an old Indian burial ground that was haunted. Yet, we were drawn to the beauty of the mountains being beckoned by the house. We did not realize we had been forewarned as we followed our heart desires!

Four years previously, we had been living in the sunny state of Florida. We were considering a move to the Rocky Mountain state to work for a Utah company. One night just before the move, I had a horrible dream about my husband.

In that dream, we moved to work with the company we were considering. I saw that within five years, my husband would die of a needless heart condition. I awoke and was very alarmed. I discussed my dream with my husband but he thought it was just a bad dream and not to worry.

We made the move to Utah and went to work for the new company. The dream was forgotten as we got on with our lives. We purchased a beautiful A-frame house nested midway up a mountain overlooking a fertile valley basin. This was our dream home and we both loved it very much.

Three years and eleven months later, the dream became a reality! My husband died suddenly from a massive heart attack. We did not even know he had a heart condition. He had been ill for the prior five or six months and the doctors were trying to figure out what was wrong with him.

During my husband's illness, we had moved him from the upstairs master bedroom down to the living room next to the stone fireplace. It was easier to heat the first floor than the entire house during the winter months. It was easier to care for him since he was now close to the kitchen and bathroom for convenience.

After my husband died, I had planned to remain in the house but after eight months I had no choice but to move closer to town. Prior to my move, at 10:30 P.M. one evening, a special picture I had made for my husband suddenly fell off the wall and crashed to the floor. The picture did not break and had never fallen before. My husband had been pronounced dead at 10:30 P.M. at the local hospital. But other then that, I could find no relationship to that incident.

Another time, a strange occurrence happened at 5:00 P.M., when the mountain silence was distrupted by a loud horrible crash. The sound had come from outside the house. My husbands van, which had been parked on the level driveway for the last year, suddenly rolled backwards down the long incline. The van crashed into a cement planter with such impact that the locking gas cap was hurled some distance from the van. The van was still in first gear and the hand brake was still set!

Then, the lady I had rented the apartment over the garage to had suddenly moved out while I was out of town. She said she had become frightened of the house and could no longer live there. I could not understand why she had moved without notice and why she became so frightened.

A year later I move from the state but I still felt connected to that house. I still had desires to go back and see it. A friend who lived in the area called one night and said there had been a bad fire at my old house. He sent the newspaper clippings so I could read what had happened.

The local paper had covered the fire. The new owners were spending the Christmas holidays in their little hideaway. Their thoughts were upon the powdery snow falling outside, skiing, relaxing by the fireplace, Christmas Carols and presents and all the joys of Yuletide. They sensed nothing out of the ordinary inside or outside of the home. Suddenly the back of the house was an inferno as a massive ball of fire went from the back of the house to the front and up to the second floor.

It seems no one had been hurt, but the house sustained extensive damage except the front living room which remained intact. The cause was a gas leak from the propane tank caused from the recent heavy snows that froze the line.

The newspaper suggested that the area may be haunted. The article in the newspaper stated the new owners had encountered so many mysterious problems after purchasing the house, they felt like 'someone didn't want them there'.

A few months later, I paid my final respects to my once old beautiful chalet. The fire had gutted only the inside my former abode. All that remained standing was the stone chimney and the colonial blue outer walls with the off-white trim. It struck me as I reread the article in the newspaper about the fire that the only room spared from damage was the living room where my husband had spent the last months of his mortal life.

Before departing, I shot a roll of film, capturing the last images of that house as a final memory of what had been. After returning home, I sent the film out for processing and printing. Upon receipt of the film from the photo lab, I discovered to my horror that none of the images had printed.

My film was ruined, as if a light source had gotten into the sealed canister and exposed the film. Yet, the entire roll of film was not ruined, only the frames in the middle of the roll that were taken of the house.

On this trip, I had shot sixteen rolls of film. However, of the 576 frames, only the shots of the house came back ruined. All of the hundred's of rolls of film that I had shot that year were developed and printed without problems, except the frames of my old house. Perhaps someone was telling me that there is nothing left for me there. I no longer have a desire to go back and visit the house or do I feel connected to it any longer.

**If you realize that all things change,
there is nothing you will not try to hold on to.
If you aren't afraid of dying,
there is nothing you can't achieve.**

**Trying to control the future
is like trying to take the master carpenter's
place.
When you handle the master carpenter's tools,
chances are that you'll cut your hand.**

**Tao Te Ching
Verse 74**

HAUNTED HOUSE ON SYCAMORE STREET

I'll begin by saying that kids growing up in my neighborhood in the 1950's were fearless. We roamed the streets and alleyways without fear. We marked our territory and knew every inch around us including every shortcut home and every hiding place. We felt as kids today feel, indestructible, immortal, tough enough to handle any situation that should come our way.

We had our favorite places to play, letting our imaginations take over completely. For me, the garage roof was a place I frequented and the best place for an afternoon being Zorro! For a time of feeling our nerve endings jump, my friends and I would trek down to the end of Sycamore Street, to 'the old house'.

Of course we had been forbidden by our parents from going down there, saying, "it wasn't safe." Even deliberate disobedience won out on occasions and we'd find ourselves being drawn to the curiosity of the old deserted house.

It was spooky in its own right but being surrounded by an old, unkept grove gave more substance to what our imaginations proclaimed, 'it was haunted', we all agreed so of course that made it definite.

The house stood alone in its majesty at the end of the street. The house sat back off the road, to be accessed only by the dirt driveway. I never recalled seeing lovely gardens with arrays of flowers blooming along the front steps, or green grass giving the place some life.

What I recall, from a child's eyes, are the remains of what had once been, long before my time. The shrubs, that once flourished, were withered and would break with a touch. The grass that had once been damp with morning dew and green as emeralds had turned to dust. It was truly left in a deathly state, which its only purpose now was to enhance the overall feeling, the house was haunted.

The old wooden house itself was yellowed with age, a two-story structure, loomed over the remains of an once prospering orange orchard. The paint was peeling away, the windows dark with caked on grime giving me the feeling though I couldn't see in, surely someone or something could see out.

The big front steps were deteriorating badly and even creaked and groaned beneath my weight. My fascination grew and my desire to tour the inside became increasingly insistent.

I had heard things coming from the house, just ordinary sounds that were enough to scare me away at a hard run. I was tough, remember? I had to know what ghostly inhabitants dwelled within those dark walls.

The tale went around that a man had hanged himself in the house and that he still walked the halls, especially from sunset to the break of dawn. Be it fact or not, the legend fit the scene and convinced us the empty old house held a dark and mysterious past and an active presence.

Darkness held us back from walking to the end of Sycamore Street, along with the fact that we were not allowed out after dark. I promised myself, before the next sunset, I would enter the house, to see for myself if the rope with the noose in the end still hung from the rafters and if the man truly roamed the house.

Surely there would be evidence of such a thing, proof the house was haunted. Since no one dared enter the place, I bolstered myself up to go in, expecting the unspeakable. Even as a child, I knew the importance of insurance so I made certain two of my friends would remain outside, within earshot, just in case I needed backup.

The day came, anticipation was high in the three of us. We had told no one of our plans, it was a 'top secret assignment'. Once the deed was done, we'd reveal the mystery of the old house to everyone, gaining recognition for bravery. We'd be the talk of the town, idols to our peers. There was no turning back, we'd worked ourselves into a state that required us to follow through, no matter what.

The afternoon grew late, it was time to go. We began slowly, nervously walking down Sycamore Street. Although it was my first experience with weakening knees, I'd never have admitted I was scared. I was the oldest, I had to set the example of fearlessness for the younger two girls. If they sensed my fear, they wouldn't want to go and I needed them with me, just in case.

We were oblivious to the normal sounds and activities of the neighborhood, caught up in discussion of the 'place'. We reached the end of the street. We stopped to look around us, making certain no one was watching. Seeing no one on the street, we proceeded down the unpaved dirt driveway.

The trees seemed to be larger and darker. Suddenly, it was quiet, too quiet and unnerving. We went on, proceeding cautiously, now aware of every sound. We felt all alone, isolated from the security of the neighborhood.

This was outside of our normal territory, not far yet isolated. The house sat empty, alone amongst the trees and suddenly there it was before us, waiting. We walked on, the only sound was that of dirt crunching under our feet with every step.

Approaching the front porch the conversation turned to every possible excuse as to why we should leave and not go in. We must have stood there five minutes, bickering back and forth. Being daring and knowing the other two would leave and I'd be left there all alone, I stated boldly, "I am going in." I climbed the front steps, they groaned under my feet. At the top step, I turned to look back, my friends anxious and whispering, "Hurry."

Facing the front door, the window to the left was the only means of entrance. It was left unlocked. I had tested it before, but hadn't dared to lift it to climb through.

As I stepped toward the window, I suddenly noticed something odd. The window was halfway open. I tingled, then realized it must be an omen, the house awaited me, it knew I was coming! I turned and ran back to my friends, my heart racing, palms sweating. "The window is open. It expected me to come today." I said to my friends.

The responses were 'go on, hurry up'. I retraced my steps back onto the front porch. I slowly edged my way to the open window, my mind wild with what I would find once inside. The curtains on either side of the window inside the room were yellowed and grimy, a strange smell drifted out which I could not identify. Fully prepared mentally to embark on the greatest adventure of my young life, I bent low to crawl through the open window. I caught sight of something moving, toward me. A gray mess, my face just in front of the gap in the window, I froze.

Whatever it was, it was coming out, I couldn't

move. A face, I saw a face then a leg coming out. I screamed and heard a hard thud. Frozen in place, I screamed again. The gray form kept coming toward me. A ghost, it had to be the ghost of the hanged man!

He stood before me, towering over my small figure, then he rubbed his head! Rubbing his head? Then he spoke, "What are you doing here? This old place isn't safe to play in, go on home."

It wasn't the spirit of the hanged man who resided within the 'haunted house', it was the owner of the company hired to tear the house down the next day. Not only would the house be leveled, but the old grove would be torn out too. The college in town had bought the land on which to build dormitories for the students.

I never learned what secrets the old house held, nor did I ever see the beckoning interior. I never forgot the experience or the feelings that accompanied the idea of 'ghost hunting'.

Through the years, I'd find myself listening to other peoples stories of haunting and ghostly activities and those sensations would return to engulf and entrance me. Who knows what was really held within those walls. After all, this was the old deserted house at the end of Sycamore Street.

HISTORY OF ASTORIA

The following stories' take place in and around the area of Astoria, Oregon which is a small seaport town at the mouth of the Columbia River and the cold Pacific Ocean. This Pacific Northwest seaport has a long and interesting history, beginning when Lewis and Clark arrived in the area in November 1805 and constructed Fort Clatsop in December 1805. Fort Clatsop was established as the winter quarters during the wet and stormy winter months until Lewis and Clark made the decision to begin their trip eastward in late March 1806 for their 'homeward journey'.

The City of Astoria is crisscrossed with a vast network of underground tunnels that have been long abandoned. These underground tunnels are the remnants of former days stores and streets before the great fires that consumed much of the city. Access to the underground tunnels of Old Town Astoria is through the many dark and spooky downstairs hallways, littered with debris from years of abandonment. Eerie dark forbidding tunnels appear as unopened tombs sealed long ago by ancient masters. Lost treasures lie hidden in the maze of dark tunnels long forgotten by living men. These uninviting dark and musty old tunnels crisscross the old City of Astoria with a complex web of tunnels that weave under the current modern streets.

Some of these underground passageways have led from old taverns, such as Hazel's Bar, to the Columbia River. These old watering holes were places where patrons could get a drink, catch up on gossip and perhaps find company for the evening. Sometimes, patrons got more then they bargained for when they found themselves kidnaped and dropped through trap doors located on the floor behind the bar. Shocked, the patron was forced through dark and musty underground tunnels, guided by hard looking men holding flickering torches, until they reached the river and waiting boats. Sailing ships prepared to depart on the next high tide for the Orient with the newly shanghaied.

LIBERTY THEATER

Liberty Theater opened its door to the public for the first time on April 4, 1925. The theater promised to be a fairyland for theater goers. It was declared to be one of the most artistic theaters on the Pacific Coast. The theater charisma attracted many famous celebrities of that era, including Duke Ellington, Jack Benny, Guy Lombardo, Claude Hopkins, Paul Whiteman, Ben Berans, Little Jack Richie and Al Capone. While attending performances, these celebrities names were penciled on the walls in the downstairs dressing rooms, below the main stage.

The picturesque architectural design of the Italian Renaissance set the Astor Building apart from all others in Astoria. Twelve bright mural canvasses of Venetian scenes painted by Joseph Knowles, a nature artist, enhanced the auditorium. Framed by plaster relief arches, the windows, like paintings are linked together, giving a panoramic effect. Theater goers gazed through painted on muntins to the Grand Canal, as if they were sitting in a Venetian Palace.

This magnificently detailed theater had a fountain whose waters played about the base of a beautiful statue, foyer walls wrapped by black and gold silk velour draperies and a chandelier fifteen feet in diameter weighing two thousand pounds.

LIBERTY THEATER GHOSTS

Entering the Liberty Theater at dusk, was like stepping back in time. My first observation in this seventy-year old building was the intricate carvings above the entrance door, on the ceilings and walls. Included in the carvings are sweet Cherub-like characters and ominous demon-like faces that encompass the large chandelier in the main theater. The lights are low which enhances the age of the structure.

Once an Opera House that drew crowds of women in long dresses and men in their fancied attire, it has a long history of tragedy and despair. As a result, the Liberty Theater has a reputation with the local residents as being 'haunted'.

Paul, referred to as the longtime resident of the theater, is one of the three known ghostly inhabitants and is also the most aggressive of the trio, appearing before the employees, unexpectedly, frightening them out of their wits.

Paul appears, "unmistakable in full dress, wearing a white tuxedo and a panama hat, always bearing a grin on his face."

"He's actually quite handsome." Says Manager Leslie Kelley.

"He's a character, showing up and pulling pranks when we least expect him, frightening us."

Paul does not like to have his name discussed. When everyone has left the theater, all is quiet and the lights are low, Paul actively lets the employees know they've said too much. The doors begin to slam and noises erupt in the dark, damp basement. One night, the concrete floor in the Managers Office began to roll like incoming ocean tide in unison with loud banging. When Leslie Kelley's chair suddenly bounced off the floor, she and her friend in the office, ran screaming from the room.

A Fortune Telling machine, sitting flush against a wall, moved to the center of the hallway floor in the basement after the theater was closed down for the night, only to be discovered the next day. A five-gallon bucket, full of paint, glides as if weightless in the 'ice room' down stairs which may be Paul's domain.

It is truly an eerie place as the light is insufficient to penetrate the darkness in the corners of the odd shaped rooms and the air smells musty and thick. You feel as though you're not alone, there is someone there, watching, though in scanning the room, there is no one else there. No body can be seen, but the feeling of being watched remains very distinct. When leaving the 'ice room', the feeling weakens yet never fully goes away until leaving the theater entirely. Along with the sensations of being observed, there is a feeling of oppression and of wonder inside the building.

According to Leslie Kelley, there is another entity that may be inhabiting the 'Ice Room'. This visitor has not been observed but it's presence is often felt. The authors captured an image on infrared film that may give a clue to its identity.

Image captured on infrared film

The authors included this image since there is a fourth entity that apparently inhabits the theater. It has not been as active as the others. The 'Ice Room' is a gloomy and eerie place. That room seems cold and musty. Once while changing infrared film in total darkness, the author felt the presence of something unnatural and unsettling. It was a weird experience.

Another time, Leslie Kelley went down to the 'CO2' room to change the soda pop canisters as one canister had gone dry. She found that the knob on the cylinder had been turned off. She turned it back on and looked up at the light bulb. Suddenly, the light bulb started to unscrew from the socket. Paul was playing another prank. Leslie Kelley ran from the room.

The CO2 room in the basement.

Lily, another well-known ghostly inhabitant, lost her life inside the theater. Her seat, which she still claims as her own today, is where she perished, at the hands of someone suspected to be her husband or boyfriend. Sitting behind the unsuspecting Lily in the darkened theater, was her assailant, concealing the weapon which would end her life.

As the theater darkened, the production on stage captured Lily's attention. Then, the man that sat directly behind her slowly and silently eased forward in his seat. Suddenly the man reached inside his coat, grasping the handle of his razor sharp knife. He slowly slipped it from its hiding place and brought it up over Lily's shoulder, across the bodice of her lovely gown, and with lightning speed, back across her neck, slashing her throat. When the lights came up, Lily was dead. Today, Lily's presence does not go unnoticed in the Liberty Theater.

A man sat in Lily's seat one evening watching a movie, unaware he was in 'Lilys' seat'. It seems a sheet of clear window type glass fell from the ceiling and crashed to the right side of the aisle seat, barely missing him. There are no windows in the theater, no glass of any kind above the seat. It seems the glass pane 'appeared', above 'Lilys' seat' out of thin air, to shatter on the floor beside him. It seems Lily doesn't like men, especially sitting in her seat!

Mary, the third member of the trio of elusive ghostly inhabitants, seemingly occupies the ladies rest room, up stairs. Mary, associated with Paul in life, seems cursed to roam the hallways in death with Paul. She was one of his women.

Mary was a prostitute who worked for Paul, her Pimp. But at one point Mary tired of her life as a prostitute and told Paul she wanted out as they stood on the balcony. Unforeseen by Mary's demands to be free, Paul became very angry and reacted by throwing fear stricken Mary off the balcony in the Liberty Theater where she died.

Mary's apparition, observed in the hallway, has walked from the projection room to the ladies room. Mary appears full bodied as she walks from the balcony to the Ladies rest room. However, only her head has been seen in the large full-width mirror, midway up the carpeted ramp leading to the ladies rest room, the projectionist booth and the two balconies. Mary has long hair and it seems she is petite. Her hair hangs straight down her head, to shoulder length, though her shoulders don't appear in the mirror. The authors were able to capture an image of what we suspect is the energy field of Mary in the hallway, next to the ladies restroom. The ghostly image appears as a reverse spin vortex.

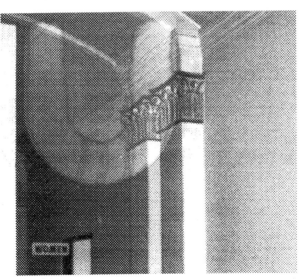

The reverse spin vortex next to Mary's Room.

Mary, too, has a special seat in the up stairs portion of the theater. Mary presides over the lounge area and the bathroom itself. She guards the stall on the right side. There are two stalls in the spacious room and both are like small rooms unto themselves. They close off completely, each having a full locking single door.

Helen Adams has experienced Mary and her antics. Mary, it seems, either likes you or she doesn't. Her way of showing how she feels about a person, is whether she locks them in her stall or not. Helen Adams is one she doesn't care for much, though we found her to be quite a pleasant lady. Helen Adams found herself locked in, by Mary.

It would have been easy to panic but knowing it would do no good, Helen Adams waited patiently until Mary decided to unlock the door and let her out. Other women have experienced the same phenomenon.

Once was enough for Helen Adams, she has avoided using the right stall, suggesting that others do similarly.

The door knob locks from the inside and not from the outside. Upon being locked in, the door knob lock was not in the locked position. However, the door knob would not turn! "The door acted like it was being held closed, by someone on the outside of the door. You can pull on the doorknob to open the door, it will open a tiny bit, but slam shut, so the only thing a person can do is sit and wait Mary out." Said Ms. Adams. Eventually, the door opens with ease.

Distinct uneasiness is the feeling that one gets when walking through the lounge area into the ladies room. The walls are red and the lights are dim, therefore, the eerie mood. It's not a place where you feel comfortable enough to go to sit and relax for a while between shows. The feeling of urgency to take care of business and leave is predominant.

After the ABC NEWS Nightline crew had completed their filming at Liberty Theater, Leslie Kelley wondered what Paul would do to show his displeasure of the film crew. Well, the staff did not have to wait long. The butter container that sits under the counter in the refreshment stand, suddenly exploded violently. A metal strip just above the butter container was hit with such violent force that a screw holding the strip in place, flew out and the metal strip was bent upward. A plastic cap, from the top of the plunger, disappeared and remains unrecovered. The hot butter spewed out all over the floor making a mess worthy of the pranks played by Paul. It is interesting since Leslie Kelley and Elena McMaster have never had any problems with the hot butter container in the past.

Elena McMaster's history lessons, included the underground passageways, accessible by old wooden doors in the theater's basement. It seems that at one time her husband had ventured from their apartment to the old Safeway store many blocks away via the underground passageway that linked their apartment house.

Leslie Kelley and Helen Adams

The Liberty Theater is for sale, it seems that the owner owns the whole block. All of the upstairs offices are vacant and bare, well we should not say bare, for there is at least one office that still has dental chairs and an old metal bucket filled with teeth.

We walked along the dark gloomy hallway connecting black vacant offices and wondered what ghostly tales they might tell. It was a dark gloomy night and it was spooky. Our flashlight was having trouble staying on. We didn't know if our batteries were going dead or if the energy fields within the building were effecting the flashlight. It frightened the living daylights out of us!

The sales price for this block of buildings is a cool one million dollars! Any takers?

SWEEPING THE FLOORS

Since my grandmother passed away, I have felt my grandmother's presence several times. It was a good feeling, like she was there to help and comfort me. Over the years whenever I would have problems to resolve, my grandmother would make a visitation and help me through the difficult times.

Later as an adult, I felt her presence and felt she was telling me "you don't need me any more." I have never felt her presence since then. Those visits were comforting by my grandmother. She helped me during my most difficult years.

Another time, my good friend and neighbor purchased a house in Astoria, Oregon which another lady had raised all her children in. After all of their children left home, her husband built a new house but this old lady did not want to move out of her old house she loved so much. She loved cleaning the house and sweeping the floors.

Finally the day came that this old lady died and my friend and neighbor bought the old house. Interesting enough, the new owner's children would often come running to their mother and tell her that they could hear a person sweeping the floor when no one was there.

Finally they got tired of having the children scared all the time by this ghost so they called someone in to rid the house of the spirit. After that ritual, the spirit never came back. At least they do not have any poltergeists busy sweeping the floor anymore.

THE BRIGHT LIGHT

Years ago, I was a kid in High School in Astoria Oregon. I would often hang out with two other boys and three girls after high school. We would often drive out to the sand dunes to have some place we could be alone. Once we parked out along the sand dunes at Fort Stevens State Park at night. We had driven out to the sand dunes in separate cars but would get into one car to talk.

While sitting in the car talking, I thought I spotted some people moving out along the sand dunes with a bright light. I wondered who would be out on the sand dunes so late at night. Whoever it was, they were too far away to clearly make out their identities.

I decided to yell at them but in doing so I got no response from them. The young women became frightened because no one should have been out on the sand dunes at this late hour. I got into my car, drove toward where I had seen the people, but when I got to the spot, no one was there. The people had vanished without a trace. The only road out was the one I was on. No other way out was possible since the sand dunes bordered on three sides by water and the road was the only way in or out. The young women became extremely scared, wondering who and what we had witnessed. I became scared and we all decided it was time to quickly depart and get back to civilization.

I got out of the service in 1969 or 1970 and I returned to Astoria Oregon. I was out at South Jetty next to the mouth of the Columbia River next to the sand dunes where I had observed some people who had vanished years before. The paved road surface was easy to travel on.

The weather was bad. It was raining and blowing like crazy. A big storm was moving into the area. It was pitch black with no moon or stars. I remember seeing a big bright light emulating from the South Jetty next to the power transformer. I couldn't believe that the light could be so bright because of the fierce storm blowing wildly.

I drove into the parking lot with my girlfriend to investigate the light source. There was something abnormal about the light that worried me. It was not a natural light and there was no source of light possible coming from the South Jetty.

I was going to get out of my car and go up over the embankment of huge boulders, hoping to see what was making such a bright light. I had gotten out of the car and was walking toward the embankment to see what was going on. My girlfriend, scared to death, did not want me to climb over the embankment of boulders. I was starting to feel uneasy and I questioned my decision to investigate the strange light so I allowed my girlfriends frantic cries of leaving to influence me.

I got back into the car, driving back around the sand dunes to the main paved road and then I exited from the South Jetty. The strange light remained visible until I drove out of sight. The weather was too stormy for boats because the waves were crashing over the embankment and over the South Jetty. I have often wondered what this strange light was and I can think of nothing that could be so bright.

Later, my girlfriend mentioned nothing of the incident. I don't know what the strange bright light was but having lived along the coast all my life, I know that no fishing boats could have survived in such rough seas. It would have been fatal to any vessels to be so close to the embankment.

THE HAUNTED PIZZA HUT

In Seaside, rumor has it that the new Pizza Hut, constructed on the property where an old house had once stood, is considered by its employees to have strange happenings when the Pizza Hut closes for the day. Apparently an old woman owned the house, until her death. Upon passing from this life to the great beyond, the property sold and the house was torn down for the construction of the new Pizza Hut.

In small towns, secrets are never secrets for long. It seems that there are rumors that when the business establishment closes for the day, with only the night staff remaining, a certain ghost will open and close doors, create noises where none should be and play general pranks. One source said that a water glass placed on the table moved all by itself. Yes, the glass actually slid across the table late one night in front of two startled employees!

It seems that some employees will play the arcade games after closing hours when it's quiet and peaceful, only to notice a 'shadow' passing behind them and when they turn to look, no one is there. Or perhaps, the doors that open and close by themselves. Typical haunting pranks were described by some of the employees.

When we asked the management about these weird happenings, they responded that they don't think they can comment on the 'ghostly' pranks. So I guess we will never know for sure, unless one wants to ask former employees about their experiences and then they will grin and start relating things that go bump in the night.

GHOSTLY IMAGES

We wondered what kind of prank would be played on us on All Halloween Eve. It was our first year in the haunted Seaside house and we suspected something out of the ordinary would happen. Our two grandchildren were visiting us, showing off their costumes. My husband had his point and shoot camera so he took some pictures of the grandchildren. These pictures were in the middle of the roll of film.

When we got our pictures back, we were shocked. The prints in the first half of the roll were just fine and the prints on the end of the roll were fine but the prints in the middle were strange.

All of the photographs taken of our two grandchildren showed some kind of mist or haze surrounding the grandchildren. It looked like some kind of energy field that completely encompassed them and nothing else. Only the images taken of them in the house were strange. Pictures of the grandchildren taken later that night outside of the house, were normal.

The above photograph is the grandson of Sharon

and Don Rogers taken in their living room. Notice the energy or plasma field surrounding the child. This photograph was taken on October 31, 1994 in the Seaside home.

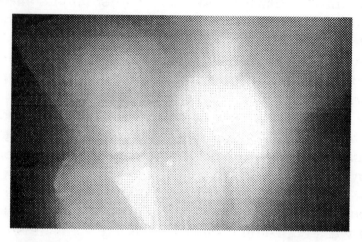

The above picture is of the two grandchildren in the Seaside home. Notice again, the plasma or energy field surrounding the children.

We showed these pictures to Dave and Sharon who wanted to use them in the book. While visiting with them, Dave used the EMF tester inside the house and found an energy field next to my husband who was sitting on the couch.

The energy field moved around his head, first from the left side then to the right side. The energy readings jumped up beyond the normal range and remained steady. This energy field was small but consistent, about the size of a football. It remained next to my husband's head.

A haunted house does not have to be a dark and gloomy place, with a sagging roof and broken windows. In Seaside, there is at least one house that is haunted by poltergeists and who knows what else!

THE MISSING BRA

I can't understand why a ghost would want to take my sports bra! Then to make matters worst, when the ghostly thief returned the bra, it wasn't even a sports bra and not in my size! Let me tell you about this strange and bizarre episode. I had gotten home from work late one night and was going to take a shower before retiring to bed. I hung up my favorite sports bra on the wall next to the shower. When I stepped out of the shower I went straight to bed. The next morning I went into the bathroom to get dressed. My new sports bra was gone!

My husband and I searched the entire house for it. Since I did not have to work for a few days, I thought perhaps my husband had decided to wash the bra and it was still in the washer or dryer. No such luck. We searched in every corner and cranny but no signs of that bra were found. I was upset at having the sports bra disappear. It was my favorite.

A few days later, my husband thought that perhaps I had tossed the bra into our bedroom closet floor and the bra had gotten buried in the heap of clothing and shoes on the closet floor. He had checked the closet floor once already but perhaps he had missed it. So he took all the shoes and clothing out from the closet and put them in a heap on the bedroom floor. Laying under the heap of clothing on the closet floor was a bra. My husband thinking he had found my bra, brought the bra out to the living room to show me. However, the bra my husband had was not my bra. That bra was too small for me to wear.

Now, if you were married and working late every night and your husband came out to the living room with a bra that didn't belong to you. You would wonder about it. I accused my husband of an affair, of having another woman in my home. I boiled over and had all kinds of wicked thoughts about my husband. I was fuming madly at him.

Well, we talked and talked and I realized how crazy my accusation of him being unfaithful to me was. I realized that I had been home since the bra was taken and the smaller bra found. There was no way a woman could have sneaked into the house while I have been here. I could not imagine how my sports bra disappeared and why the smaller bra was left in its place.

One month later, almost to the day, my new sports bra was returned to me. I was in the bedroom cleaning and moved the large crocheted bed doll. There below the doll, neatly folded, was my new sports bra. If I hadn't moved the crocheted bed doll, I would never have found it!

Our home is haunted. We have had many other experiences of ghostly pranks played on us. My husband often would be awakened at night to the sounds of someone banging on the side of the house. He would run outside and find no one around. This would occur a couple times a month between 2:00 A.M. and 3:00 A.M. but no one would ever be observed.

Other times, we hear what sounds like someone pounding on the oil tank in the basement. We had a problem with the oil furnace so we called the service man to come over and check it. He found that the wires on the furnace had been cut and rewired incorrectly. Why ghosts would want to rewire the furnace is beyond us. This is the same basement that the previous tenants experienced pranks played on their electronic circuits. The previous tenants also had photography books taken but never returned while they live here. At least my sports bra was returned.

FORT STEVENS CEMETERY

Fort Stevens Military Reservation guarded the mouth of the Columbia River from the Civil War until World War II. Fort Stevens, named for Territorial Governor General Isaac Ingalls Stevens, killed at Chantily, Virginia, in 1862, constructed during the Civil War and remained active until shortly after World War II. Today a visitor can explore the abandoned gun batteries which are the primary features of this Fort. The Fort Stevens Cemetery is located at the south end of the barracks on a dead end road.

Fort Sevens Cemetery

According to some reports, there are strange and weird happenings that are linked to the cemetery and some unmarked graves. Apparently years ago, a ship sunk in a violent storm and some bodies washed ashore. The bodies, buried in this cemetery, are in unmarked graves. It seems at least some spirits of these drowned sailors still walk the cemetery at night, at least according to the story told us by a local Astoria resident.

RINGS OF SMOKE

I purchased my first home in 1984. When I would go outside in the backyard to garden, I always got the eerie feeling someone was watching me. I would get scared and go back into the house, only to find my living room engulfed in rings of cigar smoke! I don't smoke cigars.

One afternoon, I decided to lock my front door and go outside. I was in the backyard when I again started to feel like I was being watched. I went back into the house to find rings of cigar smoke in my living room. This time I called my Mom and Dad to come up and witness this unexplained happening. They realized then that I wasn't making up the story. Mom told me to sell the house.

Another afternoon, I was sitting in my living room with my girlfriend who was visiting, along with our children. Suddenly it got dark outside, like an angry storm was brewing. An antique cup and saucer flew off my corner window sill, floated right in front of us landing upright, coming to rest on a coffee table. My girlfriend left immediately!

Strangely, that day I had received a piece of mail addressed to the man who had owned the house and had lived there for thirty-three years. In researching the man and learning some of the history, it seems that the previous owner was very ill and had shot himself. He did not die in the house but somewhere else.

People had told me that he loved his wife very much and had missed her desperatelly after she died. The man claimed to hear his wife crying in the house and calling his name from beyond the grave. The neighbors thought it was just a case of loneliness, but perhaps it was more then that.

Other times we could feel cold air come over our faces at night time, while sitting in the living room. We even had some candles go out by themselves for no apparent reason. It was spooky at times living in that house.

After we moved to Newport, Oregon our friends rented our home. They would hear a woman crying in the attic, and one night they heard sounds shuffling in the attic. The next morning they opened the attic door, and found old time baby pictures, and insulation in a heap. Unexplained antique baby pictures that were not there when we had lived in that house!

In Newport, Oregon, there are sightings of a ghost in the old lighthouse. My friend has witnessed a little girl that appeared in the lighthouse! When we investigated, there was no one in the lighthouse!

Authors Note:

The lighthouse in Newport, Oregon is the Yaquina Bay Lighthouse which was abandoned in 1874. The little girl may be Zina who was picnicking with friends. She ran back inside the building to get her gloves and never was seen again.

HISTORY OF ST. HELENS

The history of St. Helens Oregon extends back beyond a century. Lewis and Clark Expedition paddled by this land in 1805 which was uninhabited by white people. Nathaniel Wyeth arrived in 1834, to establish a fort and trading post on the lower end of Sauvie Island. Ten years later a sawmill was built near what today is St. Helens.

Capt. Henry M. Knighton arrived from Maine to file the first land claim sometime in 1846 or 1847. Knighton plotted a town he called Plymouth. Prior to his plotting the town site, the local name for the small gathering of log huts was Wyeth's Rock. The name was changed in 1850 to St. Helens.

According to an article in The Chronicle by Richard Spiro, dealing with the History of settlement of St. Helens, "The city streets were dirt, or mud, depending on the weather. In time wooden sidewalks provided a mildly civilized touch, although now and then a loose plank would fly up and smack the passerby." The following stories take place in and around St. Helens, Oregon.

THE CREAKING STAIRS

I moved to an old established farm at Deer Island, Oregon with my husband and children in about 1950. We bought it from my husbands father, who had farmed the property for years. The old farm property, homesteaded in the late 1860's as part of the Oregon Land Donation Act of 1850, was rich in local history. According to some local old time residents, the surrounding acreage next to the farmhouse had once been an old Indian village and perhaps a burial ground. It seems that each year Indian arrowheads and other related artifacts would be uncovered when the fields were plowed in preparation for crops. Well, it was shortly after we moved to that farm that the "ghostly experience" began.

Let me explain about our old farmhouse. Our home was an old time typical two-story farmhouse, built in the days when they built houses with square nails. It was a lovely white house with a woodshed next to the porch. We used to fill the woodshed with firewood cut from fallen trees we found on the timbered portion of the farm.

My husband would hitch a trailer to the tractor and head for the woods to look for fallen trees during the summer months. Our three boys would help him load the trailer with the chunks he would saw from the fallen tree.

The wood stove provided the heat for our home during the winter months. Old farm houses are hard to heat in the winter, there is not much insulation. I remember we had planted a willow twig next to the outdoor water faucet next to the woodshed.

Over the years it grew and provided us with shade during the summer and a place for our boys to climb and explore. It was also the home of many humming-birds who made their home in that willow tree. Typical with old farmhouses, all five bedrooms were located upstairs while the single bathroom was located on the main floor next to the kitchen and living room. The staircase was narrow and steep. We had a gun rack on the wall just inside the stairwell where we kept our .22-caliber rifles.

After everyone had gone to bed for the evening, the stairs creaking would awaken us. The creaking of the stairs sounded just like someone was walking down the stairs. You could hear one step after another creak, then there would be silence after the bottom step creaked.

Many a night we had gotten up and turned on the hall light thinking maybe one of our boys had gotten up and were going down the stairs but no one was ever there. If you turned on the lights while the stairs were still creaking then the noise would immediately stop and not resume until the lights were turned off. After an hour or so the creaking would start all over. However, this time the steps were creaking from the bottom to the top, one step at a time.

A funny thing--the steps never creaked in the daytime but only at night after the boys had all gone to bed. We would often joke about having some kind of house guest staying with us who always got hungry in the middle of the night. The sounds of creaking stairs never frightened us but we often wondered who was making these sounds. We never discovered the source.

THE BATHROOM MUSIC

Another strange thing that happened in this house was that occasionally day or night when the house was still you could hear faint music playing when the radio and television were off. The music was the clearest and loudest in the bathroom and seemed to be coming from the bath tub. The music could be heard for ten to fifteen minutes and then there would be complete silence. These mysterious things happened for all the years we lived in the house.

After we moved from the farmhouse, we rented out the farm house. Our renter reported that she often felt someone was watching her and once in awhile she could see a face peering in the window but before she could get a good look, the face vanished.

We then sold the farm and the next owners that lived in the farm house reported hearing the same noises that we had.

VISITORS FROM THE GRAVEYARD

We live in a haunted house that is located next to a cemetery that was established in 1906. Another cemetery, established in 1873, is not far from our home. If that is not enough, an old Indian burial ground is located not far from our home. These Indian grounds were the sites for their villages and their burial grounds. We have been told that within a quarter mile of our house is the spot used by the Indians as a gathering area for trading.

During the last six months we have felt the presence of several visitors from the cemeteries. Most of these visitors have arrived between 2:30 A.M. and 3:00 A.M. while we have been asleep. It is during this time that we are awakening to the sounds of footsteps walking from the backdoor, which faces the cemetery, to the living room. The footsteps are clearly heard, but no one is observed when we check. The footsteps are heard coming into the house but never departing. It is as if someone walks in and sits in one of our chairs.

We have heard the muffled sounds of people talking, occasionally making out a word or two. Sometimes the voices are males yet at other times they sound like men and women talking. Sometimes the sounds of the voices come from our basement while other times we can't make out where the voices are coming from.

Our den has had some strange happenings. Once a windup music box started playing. We checked it but could not decide why it started playing. It had been sitting on the shelve for over six months without playing and we had not round up the spring in the music box. Another time we left an empty plastic eight-ounce bottle of orange juice on the floor. The next morning we found the plastic bottle with about two ounces of orange juice in the bottle. Now, we know that the plastic bottle was empty when we left it on the floor. We were going to discard it the next morning when we were going to clean the den.

The fire alarm buzzer in the master bedroom will occasionally beep once about 2:30 A.M. and then remain dormant the rest of the night. This has happened about four times now. One beep only and it beeps around the same time each night. We often will be laying on the bed and will experience something jumping up on the bed. The bed will shake and then silences. It feels like a small animal like a dog or cat has jumped up to the bed. But there is no dog or cat on the bed!

A few weeks ago we were loading our recreation vehicle with some supplies so we could be gone for a few days. I was in the office making some telephone calls as my wife was carrying out some boxes of supplies to the recreation vehicle. As she walked out on the patio and headed for the recreation vehicle, she noticed a man had just walked behind the recreation vehicle. She walked to where she lost sight of the man and looked to see who was there. She could see nobody anywhere. If a person had walked behind the recreation vehicle, he would still be visible when she got to the spot he disappeared behind the recreation vehicle. Our closest neighbors were too far way for someone to have walked to in the few seconds it took her to investigate. Whoever this person was, he simply disappeared.

Now our recreation vehicle has also experienced some strange events. There is one light bulb that will come on above the cab-over bed. We never use this light and it will only come on when we leave the recreation vehicle parked for a few days. While traveling last summer for three weeks, we never had this light bulb come on by itself. We are not sure why we are having so many visitors in our home. Our house is definitely haunted!

THE RED GLOW IN THE BASEMENT

The house I grew up in is in St. Helens. It is owned by my parents who are still living in it. Our house is quite interesting. Upstairs in the bedrooms, the closet has access to an inner passage way that leads entirely around the house, accessing each closet in the upstairs bedrooms. I have often wondered if sometime in the past, the house was used to hide people. My parents have lived in that house for about eighteen years, since I was about four. As soon as we moved in eerie things started to happen. Many of the things are still blurry since I was so young.

One of the things that I do remember took place when I was seven years old. One night my mom was asleep on the couch while my step-dad was working shift work. There was a really bad thunder storm that night. We had an Alaskan Husky dog who used to always walk over to the hallway next to a corner and bark at that corner. She would also bark toward the stairs leading to my bedroom or bark at the stairs leading down to the basement. Our dog would never walk down those stairs. She would go outside and enter the basement from the outside but those stairs really scared her.

On this particular night, she was barking really loud at the corner. My mother got the impression someone was trying to pull her off the couch. The dog was standing in the middle of the room looking at her. My mom walked over to the stairs and had an overwhelming fear that something was wrong with me.

She ran up the stairs and stopped as if hitting a brick wall. She felt like someone was trying to push her down the stairs, determined, she went up the stairs and found me on the floor sleeping. She awakened me and asked what had happened. I said that I had fallen out of bed so I just stayed on the floor. Now this is the

Sharon A. Gill & Dave R. Oester

strange part. I was laying on a blanket with a pillow. I had another blanket over me that was tucked in on all sides. The bedroom window was wide open and the rain was blowing in.

However, when I went to bed that night, the window was closed! I told my mom that I had not tucked myself in on the floor. She said I couldn't have tucked myself in according to the way she saw the blankets tucked around me with my arms under the blanket. My mom sometimes would talk about seeing a blur in the corner that our dog would always bark at.

My mom would stay up all night at times, afraid of turning off the lights. She doesn't like talking about her experience because she is afraid people will think she is crazy.

My parents purchased the home from a couple whose parents had built the home. The old couple both died in the house. The man had died naturally and the old lady had fallen down the basement stairs and broke her neck.

My mom once walked into a room and thought she could smell a man's cologne. We had been gone for a few days and the house was locked up. We searched for where the cologne came from but we could never find anything.

There are many eerie and strange happenings associated with our basement. When you go into the basement, there are two doors. One is a basement door and the second door leads to the outside porch.

Downstairs are a lot of shelves for storage. Ever since I was a young kid, I have been terribly frightened of the basement. I use to have nightmares about going to the storage rooms and finding an old lady's body or heads jumping out at me.

I slept upstairs at night and if I had to go to the bathroom, I would have to walk down the stairs, go through the living room and through the kitchen, passing the basement door. I would walk by that basement door and just stare at it. I was terrified of that basement door. There were a couple of incidents where the door would open a few inches by itself, then I would go right back upstairs without using the bathroom and wet my pants because I was so terrified. My mom would have to go down with me or I would not go.

That basement door was always locked, my parents always locked it and I always checked the door on my way to bed. Yet, I have watched the basement door open slowly by itself when it should have been locked! I remember once it opened about two inches and I could see what appeared to be a red glow coming from the basement when none should have been there.

One time I was sleeping downstairs and I looked out of the bedroom I was in. I could see into the kitchen area, I could see a really bright red glow all over the kitchen. It was really spooky! I don't ever go into the basement anymore. In fact, I try not to go to that house very much if I can avoid it.

There is something very strange about that house. The lock on that basement door was the old fashion kind that one had to twist to lock, so there is no way it could open by itself.

Even today, before my parents leave the home, they make sure that the basement door is locked. I feel perfectly safe upstairs. I kind of looked on the old lady ghost as my protector probably because of being tucked in when I fell out of bed that one time. However, the things that go on downstairs are simply scary.

When I was about eighteen or nineteen and still living at home, I got into a conversation with an older gentleman about older houses and haunted houses. He knew about our St. Helens house and the old woman who died in our house. She was crippled and fell down the basement stairs and broke her neck at the bottom of the stairs. Now, I know why I have been terrified of those stairs for years. This was the old lady's ghost who we joked about while growing up.

My parents don't like to talk about the basement and the red glow. My step-dad remembers the red glow but will not talk about it even today. My aunt stayed with us for a short time and she swears she saw objects levitate in the air. My parents often joke about objects that are moved in the house. My mom often says that the old lady is rearranging the house again when objects are moved.

We have had several incidents involving having strangers in the house. Once I went down to the basement, a hairy man was in the basement and followed me up the stairs but I locked the door and locked him in. We called the police but they could find nothing and we could find no tools or anything missing.

Another time my mom and brother were watching television in the living room. They had turned off all of the lights in the other rooms except the living room. My brother had fallen asleep while watching video movies. When he woke up he noticed the light in the kitchen was on and heard a noise in the kitchen. He awoke my mom and she walked toward the kitchen.

Suddenly, a hairy arm came around the corner and turned off the light switch on the wall next to the kitchen. My brother said that the arm was a man's arm and very hairy. I often wonder if that hairy arm and the hairy man I saw in the basement were the same.

I was not home at the time. But another time, my parents had company over for the evening when they all heard music coming from my upstairs bedroom. Someone was turning the volume up and down on the radio.

They were afraid to enter the room to investigate. They called the police but they could find no one in the room. The windows were opened in the room.

Nothing was stolen from the room, only the radio was disturbed by adjusting the sound levels. The radio was turned off by the time they got upstairs to check.

Today, I make sure that all my doors are locked and I am still afraid of that basement door. I don't know what was making the red glow but I don't want to know.

There are some things better to be left unexplored. I am terrified of being alone because of those early experiences. I have a specific place for everything. This way, I will know if anything has been moved.

I've had to leave my radio on after I moved out of the house because I needed to have sound coming in to block out the eerie sounds of that house. I have had sleeping problems over the years I know are a direct result of that house.

Now, I am a very light sleeper, I can hear any noise that is out of place during the night. I have not tried to learn what actually took place in that house. Somethings are better left undisturbed. I believe this is one of them.

GHOSTLY GUESTS

The first time I had strange experiences happen is when I lived up on Pittsburg Road in St. Helens. I had my father-in-law, my two brothers-in-law, my sister-in-law, their three kids, my husband, myself and my son, all living in a one and half bedroom house. I was working graveyard down at Boise-Cascade as a security officer.

My father-in-law would always have my meals prepared for me when I came home from work or when I got ready to go to work. I came home from work one morning and ate breakfast. Everybody else in the house had already eaten so all their dishes had already been washed and put away. The only thing left in the sink was my glass and my plate.

We were all sitting in the front room talking, the kids were all outside playing. Suddenly we heard this crash in the kitchen. Upon checking the source of the noise, I found my plate that I'd left in the sink, was now on the kitchen floor, broken. I had decided that the house was haunted so I moved but the ghost moved with us.

I moved to another house in Deer Island. Little strange things began to happen again, like I'd set something down on the counter and in returning for it, it would be gone. Nobody was in the house but me. I decided maybe it was time to move again.

I then moved to another home. My husband had died in October 1988. My daughter was two years old at the time and my son was living with me at the time. We set up a Christmas tree in the living room. My little daughter's ornament fell off the tree and rolled across the floor. The kids were in bed and the cat was outside. I would pick up the ornament and hang it back on the tree, then shortly, the ornament would fall off the tree again and roll across the floor.

The next day a friend was visiting with me. We were sitting at the kitchen table. There was a sack of potatoes sitting on the kitchen floor next to the utility room, ready to be put away. One of the potatoes had fallen out of the sack and rolled across the kitchen floor.

So I picked up the potato and put it back into the sack and then pulled up the edges of the sack. About half hour later, that same potato rolled across the floor for the second time! I decided it was time for dinner so I cooked that potato we ate it to be rid of it.

I then moved to Columbia City, two miles north of St. Helens, into my mom's hundred year old home which badly needed remodeling. I had remarried and my new husband, a truck driver, was not a very handy person when it came to carpenter tools.

His father, who had died of cancer had been a carpenter all his life and was very good at working with tools. The house required a lot of work. New insulation had to be installed, new siding had to replace the old shiplap that had originally been used.

Well, we started the remodeling process and it was hard work. The house was old and all of the walls were crooked, only one wall in the entire house was straight. My husband was doing all of the repairs and remodeling and doing a fantastic job. Every board he cut to redo the walls fit perfectly! He often exclaimed, "I'm not that good of a carpenter!" We have a feeling that his dad helped him do the carpenter work and his spirit is now living with us.

We still have our previous 'guest' from my former home still living with us. My husband would lay down his tape measure and come back for it in a few minutes but it would be gone. He would leave and come back and the tape measure would be where he originally left it.

I had put my car keys in my purse one night, I

went to get them the next morning and they were gone. I dumped my purse out on the floor, spilling the entire contents on to the floor and no keys! I picked up everything on the floor and put them back into my purse and set it on the table and went outside. Later I remembered something I wanted from my purse, I opened the purse to find my keys on top of the contents.

We have a blind black cat that will act funny at times. Since he is blind, his other senses are more acute. He will walk across the front room floor and then he'll jump over something invisible to us in the middle of the floor. There is nothing on the floor for the cat to jump over. Once we noticed his whiskers will twitch like there is something messing with his whiskers but there is nothing there that we can see.

Once my little dog, named Charlie, would go running through the house, suddenly he would stop and turn around and look like something was chasing him, but there is nothing there. Like I said, whenever I move, my ghost will move with me to my new home, sometimes I wish they would stay behind and bless somebody else.

HAUNTING "666" MYSTERY

Once we got our home in Columbia City remodeled, my husband and I turned back to driving trucks again to earn a living. We are both professional truck drivers. I don't know how to describe the next experience, it was bizarre.

When my husband and I first started driving the truck over the road, we had a 1988 black Kenworth that was given to us. It was brand new, no mileage on the thing. We had a speedometer and a hubometer and whenever the mileage would roll over, on either one of them to '666', something would happen that day. It never failed.

One time we were in Portland with my old GMC that I had. I was driving it and was told to pick up a container, number '666'. I told my boss I wouldn't go pick it up as number '666' is the mark of the devil. I said, "I don't want that trailer." He said I had to take it to Longview, Washington. I finally said, "Okay, I'll take it but I have warned you not to be surprised should something happen today." I took the container to Longview.

Upon returning to Portland, I blew out a tire. When I got into the rail yard, I had disconnected my lines, I know I had disconnected the lines off of my truck. I went to pull away and my emergency line was still hooked up to my truck and busted.

I know I had disconnected that line because I had tripped over the stupid line when I pulled them off and laid them on the decking of my truck. I have no idea how the line was reconnected to my truck. It is something I cannot explain.

GHOSTLY MUSIC

I lived in St. Helens with my husband and our two children. My son Joe was twelve years old and my daughter was fourteen years old at the time these things took place.

We moved into the house the first week in November of 1988 and stayed for five weeks before we moved out because of the ghosts. Our first experience began just before Christmas. When we first moved in, little things would happen, just to make you wonder, like what was that?

One time I sat on my bed. I was doing something at the night stand when suddenly from behind me on the bed, I felt the sensation of a cat or something that had jumped on the bed and laid down beside me. Now, we didn't own a cat, so I turned around to look and nothing was there. Not even an indentation on the bed. I could feel the sensation that something was there. I had felt the bed move but nothing was there.

Another thing that happened and is kind of hard to explain. In the bathroom, where the faucet comes out to the bathtub, my husband had installed a new faucet. The old metal washer was flush up against the wall. He had tightened it with a pipe wrench. I had watched him tighten that metal washer.

Two or three days later, he was at work and the kids were at school. I was in the bathroom and when I looked at the faucet that metal washer was loose looking. I touched it because it should not have been loose. I flicked it with my finger and it turned. It was loose! I thought that was really weird. Later in the afternoon, I returned to the bathroom and was wondering about that washer. I reached over to spin the metal washer again but this time it was tight and would not move!

Another time, I was sitting in the living room

watching television; it was probably around ten or eleven in the morning. The kids were at school and my husband was at work when I heard this noise that sounded like the 'chink' sound made by metal chains being moved. The sound was loud enough to be heard over the television set and loud enough for me to turn and look around trying to find where the sounds were coming from.

All of these little things just kept adding up but I never said anything to anyone because I didn't know if it was just me or what! My husband went out of town for a couple of weeks. He had a job in Astoria. The first night he was out of town was the first night he'd ever been away from us. The kids went to bed around 9:30 P.M. so I went in my bedroom and laid down.

The kids wanted to sleep downstairs. A lot of times they wanted to sleep downstairs anyway because they didn't like it upstairs. The living room had two couches, a television and a stereo. Each of my children were sleeping on separate couches.

About twenty minutes later, I was almost asleep when the sound of a live band blasted from the living room. I thought Joe had turned on the stereo system so I hollered, "Joe, turn the stereo off!" The sounds of the music had awakened my children and Joe yelled back, "Mom, the stereo is not on." I am screaming at him because this music is loud. When he yelled to me that it was off, I yelled to him, "What do you mean the stereo is not on?" I yelled for him to unplug it and Joe said it was unplugged.

Our old stereo was normally left unplugged unless it was in use. The only way to turn on the stereo system was to plug it in and to turn it off we unplugged the cord.

When Joe had said it was unplugged, I got goose bumps in places I didn't know I could get goose bumps. I got up from bed and went downstairs to the living room to investigate what was happening. By that time, the kids were standing up.

There is this sound of a live band in our living room. All of a sudden, the music kind of dwindled off into the kitchen area. We followed the sound of music into the kitchen. The music was just as loud in the kitchen as it has been in the living room.

I picked up a frying pan, my son grabbed a baseball bat and my daughter grabbed a kitchen knife. Now the music had left the kitchen area and was now at the foot of the stairs. As soon as we walked past the bathroom and approached the stairs, the music suddenly stopped. There was dead silence in the house.

The music had definitely come from within the house. The sound didn't come from the outside of the house or by someone walking by while playing a 'boom box' on their shoulder, it was definitely inside!

We went back to bed, the kids got in bed with me along with the frying pan, the baseball bat and the kitchen knife. I laid there in bed for a minute, thinking we should get out as there was something going on that wasn't right. So we got up and stayed the night over at my sister's house. I had by that time become really freaked out and refused to go home until my husband returned. My sister's husband went back to our place and picked up some clothes for the kids. I wasn't going back into that house without my husband.

I talked to my husband on the phone but I didn't tell him what had happened. He was involved in a really tedious job and I didn't want him worrying or upset on the job so I didn't say anything to him at the time.

After a few weeks, I began to think that perhaps I had overreacted and it was silly of me to act this way. I asked my dad to go over to the house and check out the electricity in the house. He suggested perhaps it had been a power surge. I don't accept this explanation because it sounded like a live band.

I was beginning to feel like a 'big chicken', so we went back home. Nothing happened the first night. However, the second night after we had done some last minute shopping for Christmas at Payless Drugs we arrived home in the cold and dark about seven and walked into the house. After setting our packages down on the desk Joe went straight to the bedroom and shut the door but the door didn't shut all the way. He walked over to the bed and before he could sit on the bed, he yelled, "Something just hit me in the back."

He ran out of the bedroom and I said, "What do you mean, something hit you in the back?" I thought maybe someone was in the bedroom. He said he didn't know, he was crying and pulling off his coat. I helped him take his coat off and on his right shoulder blade was a red welt. I said to Brenda, "Look at this!" Then the initial 'J', all white, raised above the red welt.

It was quite prominent. I can't describe exactly how I felt, I had to reach over to get my purse so I could get my car keys and I could hardly move. I grabbed my purse and the kids and I took off outside.

We jumped in the car and started to leave. As we were driving away, I glanced back at the house and upstairs, in Brenda's bedroom, her whole bedroom was lit up, the front window and the side windows. It was lit up like someone left a light on. The only problem, there had been no light fixtures in her bedroom but the whole room was lit up. There wasn't even a lamp in her room.

She rarely stayed upstairs, as I said they didn't like it up there so they mostly stayed downstairs. I never set foot in that house again! We moved to another house in the area, away from that part of town.

ST. HELENS SENIOR HIGH SCHOOL GHOST

St. Helens, Oregon is a sleepy little rural town which is located north of Portland along the Columbia River. The town of St. Helens is steeped in history stemming from the time of the Lewis and Clark Expedition of 1805 when they paddled past this future town site. Heavy timber attracted the loggers who built up the town and established a port to ship harvested lumber to the hungry markets of the east.

Here, in this small town, lives a most interesting poltergeist named Vera. The myriad of pranks that have been experienced by the various staff members and students of the high school are being credited to a poltergeist that the school members have named Vera.

This ghost story is supposed to have began at the turn of the century. It seems that Pacific University in Forest Grove, Oregon had a music student murdered in the music building late one night. Her name was Vera and she is said to have haunted the music building of that university for years. Supposedly, her murder is still unsolved by the local law enforcement agencies.

However, Pacific University still claims that the ghost of Vera still walks the hall of their University and did not make the journey to St. Helens. The apparition of Vera still appears from time to time at Pacific University. They suggest that St. Helens Senior High School has picked up their own ghost since Vera is still very active at Knight Hall. See the Pacific University version in the newspaper article published in The Oregonian, entilted 'Portlandgeist', included in another section of this book and the story entiled 'Knight Hall Ghost'.

The St. Helens version of our story starts in 1983 when the High School Drama Department was preparing to perform the Music Man production. The Drama

Department needed band uniforms, so they arranged to borrow band uniforms from Pacific University in Forest Grove, Oregon.

According to the high school folklore, in the process of moving the band uniforms to St. Helens, Vera is said to have apparently decided to follow the uniforms and became a resident poltergeist (a ghost that makes noises but does not show itself) of the St. Helens Senior High School Auditorium.

The author had been told that about five or six years ago there was an article written on Vera by a reporter for the Chronicle, the local newspaper. The author decided to brave the weather and attempt to research that article. The author arrived at the newspaper office and was shown to a table while the receptionist hefted two large red bounded volumes containing all of the newspapers for 1989.

The author slowly thumbed through each page, looking for any articles written on a ghost named Vera. The author discovered the death notices for his father, Raleigh Robert Oester, who had passed away on January 5 of that year from cancer. The author reflected on his father's death and wiped away a tear and got back to the business at hand, scanning each page for information about a ghost named Vera. When finished I asked for the next two bound volumes for 1988. Fortunately luck was on my side since I had only to thumb through newspaper pages from January 1 to March 16, 1988.

Then I discovered the elusive article on the ghost Vera written by Reporter Jeri Lessard, published on Wednesday, March 16, 1988 by The Chronicle entitled, 'Ghost' plays pranks on thespians, guards Olmscheid stage. The newspaper article clearly tells an interesting story which we have included. The newspaper article is used with permission of The Chronicle.

I quote, "A light flickers off and on without an

electrical source, and a piano that plays although no one is there. The distant hammering of nails can be heard but the doors are locked and you know you are the only one in the building.

Or are you really alone?

Perhaps it's just a mischievous spirit just over your shoulder - a ghost which is unable to rest because of an unsolved murder. Then again, perhaps the noises and flickering lights can be attributed to an active imagination or a quick-moving prankster.

Olmscheid Auditorium, St. Helens High School's 500-seat facility, reportedly houses a ghost which local Thespians have named Vera. Believers say she has been playing pranks, particularly during play rehearsal, for nearly five years.

"Supposedly, every auditorium should have a ghost," said Cheri Adams, high school drama teacher. Olmscheid inherited its spirit, in the summer 1983 during the Shoe String Community Players production of "The Music Man."

John Schmor, as director of the production, borrowed band uniforms for the occasion from Pacific University in Forest Grove. The uniforms were stored in the university's music building, Knight Hall, which is said to be haunted by a young music student named Vera who was murdered at the turn of the century.

Legend has it that Vera was the daughter of a past university president and was killed either in a 19th-century Indian massacre or by an ungracious suitor. On the other hand, Peggy Cadd, administrative assistant at Knight Hall, said no facts exist to confirm Vera's existence.

Schmor attributed mysterious happenings at Olmscheid to the university's ghost, which came to St. Helens with the band uniforms.

Heather Jester, a high school student who worked backstage during the play, "Fools" in the spring 1987, recalls fixing a staircase on the set just before the production's closing night. Although the young woman was sure she was alone in the auditorium, Jester noticed "Vera's light" came on - a particular stage light which is known for turning off and on even though the theater's computerized lighting system has been unplugged.

"All of a sudden, the piano started playing," Jester said. She stepped toward the nearby piano, but saw no one there. She is convinced there was not sufficient time for a prankster to run away. Jester left the auditorium abruptly and didn't return until other thespians had arrived.

In the most recent high school production, students' Chris Johnson and J. Wright were rehearsing for "Brighton Beach Memoirs" on the unlighted stage. Cox went off to find keys to the booth which hold the lighting system. "I was thinking it was getting hard to read, and it would be nice to have some light," Wright claimed. Before Cox could obtain the keys, Vera's light mysteriously switched on.

The students noted Vera's light once blinked off and on wildly during a high school assembly regarding teen-age suicide.

Adams said electricians have inspected the lighting system on numerous occasions but cannot discover anything wrong. She also once heard unexplained footsteps across the stage, but attributes such phenomenons to a new building which settles and shifts during the heating and cooling process. "A lot of it is the power of suggestion," Adams said concerning the ghost stories.

Nick Federici, 1985 graduate of the local high school, attributes a frightening experience from the fall 1983 production of "Dracula" to the power of suggestion.

He returned to the dark auditorium to retrieve

some items belonging to a fellow cast member, who had run screaming from the stage after hearing mysterious footsteps. "It's the spookiest feeling that I have ever felt. I leaned over to pick the item up and felt like there was someone right behind me," Federici explained.

An unusual photograph also has been attributed to Vera over the years.

During the high school spring musical "Seven Brides for Seven Brothers" in the spring 1986, Mike Welch was taking photographs of scenes from the play. Welch, who owns a local photo processing shop, said either he or his daughter Courtney snapped a picture with an "unexplained light mark." The greenish swirl, apparently in motion from left to right, seemed to encircle a cast member on the color print.

Courtney Welch saw the photograph and told her father that it was Vera herself. "I didn't have a ready explanation for it. I still don't," Mike Welch said.

"There are lots of things happen in photography that I can't explain," Mike Welch added. He said the green mark could be attributed to a "lens flare," in which light enters the camera lens at an unusual angle and leaves a unique mark on the negative. The photo technician said a lens flare was possible particularly with the colored lights used on the stage. He called the unusual light "a curiosity and a coincidence," while his daughter called the green shape Vera.

Whether logical explanation, coincidence or the supernatural, the high school Thespians hold to their belief in the auditorium ghost. One student said, "strange things happen" if Vera is not given credit in a theatrical production at Olmscheid. Therefore, her name is mentioned faithfully in each program.

Such faith goes beyond the high school students, Bill Cade, co-founder of Shoe String Players, said he greets Vera whenever he enters the auditorium . . .

If you don't greet her, she will inevitably do something to cause chaos.

Cade disagreed with the description of Olmscheid's ghost as mischievous, but said the spirit has a love of theater. "She just cares about us. She's just the grand overall caretaker of the auditorium." End of quote.

The authors attempted to follow up leads from the newspaper article by contacting Mike Welch who supposedly had a photograph of Vera. Unfortunately, his wife said they did not have time to search through the many files containing photographs.

We tried to contact Bill Cade concerning his version of the events that took place. We left a message on his answering machine asking to be called back. We left the message that we were ghost writers and that ABC NEWS Nightline was coming from New York to do a story on us and we wanted to include the Vera story.

We were told later that Mr. Cade did not take our request to interview him seriously and wrote us off as pranksters. It seems he did not believe ABC NEWS Nightline was coming to St. Helens to do a story. We were successful in contacting Cheri and Rolf Adams who were more than happy to discuss Vera.

Rolf Adams, substitute teacher and husband to Cheri Adams, clearly believes that the poltergeist pranks played on the Drama students should be credited to Vera. Rolf Adams feels very protective of their schools ghost, especially to 'outsiders'. The authors have found this 'protective' characteristic to be common in incidences where poltergeist activities are strong and associated with playful but not harmful pranks.

According to Cheri Adams, high school drama teacher, Vera stays in the Auditorium and does not visit other portions of the school. She says for some reason Vera prefers the Auditorium. When asked if many of her students have had experiences with Vera, she responds that usually freshmen coming in to her class will not have had experiences but by the time they are seniors, they are normally believers.

Cheri Adams with Auditorium in background

We had an opportunity of sitting with Dean Ebert, an admitted skeptic who works the graveyard shift at the high school as a custodian. He says strange things do happen during the night. He recounted hearing a piano playing in a locked vacant room, of lights coming on and spotlighting him in the stage area. Then there are the rooms that are locked with their lights turned off and later when the custodians return, they will find the room door open and the lights on. These pranks have occurred throughout the school, not just in the auditorium.

Ebert states that many of his associates on the custodial staff have had to work up courage to visit the Auditorium where Vera haunts, especially the new members working the graveyard for the first time. However, being a skeptic does not keep him from referring to her as Vera whenever he is asked about some of his strange encounters.

Dean Ebert being interviewed by Kathy Kennedy

It seemed that most students we had a chance to talk with were familiar with the story of Vera and at least some of her pranks especially the blinking of the stage lights in the Auditorium. These students accepted the stories of Vera as part of their heritage at the high school.

They often smiled as we discussed some of the pranks credited to this poltergeist. However, there are some students who claim the ghost Vera is a hoax and is being perpetrated by the drama department and that the ghost does not really exist in their high school.

Those nonbelieving students may be considered the true skeptics. Perhaps, until they too experience the poltergeist pranks such as the sounds of spooky footsteps in an empty room, phantom piano music being played in locked rooms or the blinking on and off of the stage lights in response to the name Vera being spoken.

Other sources have claimed that perhaps the poltergeist was a prior student who had committed suicide at the school because of a tragic love affair. Apparently this poltergeist plays pranks on people in other parts of the building not related to the drama department. Lights are turned on and off, doors open and close by themselves. It seems one thing is sure, there is one or more poltergeist present in the St. Helens Senior High School.

As of yet, no ghostly apparitions or phantoms of the ghost Vera have been reported by the staff members or by the many Thespian students who believe she exists. Perhaps Vera is too shy for that kind of appearance on stage. Then again, perhaps Vera may be a former student who haunts the school looking for his lost love. Time will tell . . .

VERA OF PACIFIC UNIVERSITY

Vera, the resident ghost of Knight Hall is alive and well on Pacific University Campus in Forest Grove, Oregon. Knight Hall is an old 19th century structure that was the music department for many years until the music department was moved to another building. Knight Hall is now the Admissions Office for Pacific University. Many hoped that Vera would follow the music department in their move but alas this was not the case.

Vera decided to remain in Knight Hall and now haunts the Admissions Office. Vera has been haunting Pacific University for over fifty years and the students and staff members love it. Vera is honored from time to time by the students by holding a sleep over in Knight Hall.

Knight Hall, Pacific University

The authors were contacted by NBC Good Evening in late December 1994 and asked if we could line up another haunted house story that they could film in January 1995. We suggested the resident ghost called Vera of Pacific University. NBC Good Evening liked the Vera ghost idea so we scheduled with Pat Kosharek of the Admissions Office to do a story on Vera. According to Pat Kosharek, Admissions Counselor, Vera is the resident ghost of Knight Hall which is now used as the Admissions Office.

Pacific University is a small town University located in rural Forest Grove, Oregon. This 1849 chartered University was founded by Congregational pioneers. It started out as Tualatin Academy and later became a missionary college for the Congregational Church. Old College Hall, Pacific's first classroom building was erected in 1850 for the Tualatin Academy, making it one of the oldest educational buildings in the western United States.

The friendly atmosphere abounds here as one walks along the pathways within the campus. The various students we came into contact with were friendly and open and spoke highly of their resident ghost Vera. The staff members of the Admissions Office were more then helpful in assisting us gather information on their ghostly inhabitant.

They even offered to allow us to stay all night in Knight Hall so we could experience the ghostly pranks of Vera. No one we spoke with felt ashamed or embarrassed that we were there to search for Vera. They spoke about Vera's activities without fear, as though she is a normal part of their daily lives. It truly was refreshing and gives credit to the University for their open minded attitude when dealing with paranormal events.

The legend has it that the building, named Knight Hall, is haunted by a singing and whispering ghost named Vera. Many stories have emerged over the years about who Vera was and how she died. Some say she was the daughter of John Herrick, the University's second president. Others say she was a music student who either died in the building by accident or by committing suicide. Still others says the mysterious Vera was killed in an Indian massacre, while others say she was murdered by her lover.

Unfortunately, none of the stories can be proven at this time but nevertheless Vera is legendary throughout Oregon. It is not uncommon for Portland radio stations to broadcast from the Knight Hall on October 31. KEX was one such station who decided to broadcast their Halloween Night program from a real haunted house, they chose Pacific's Knight Hall. DJ Francine Raften spent five long hours in the building with a woman who claimed to be a medium and with several KEX broadcast personalities.

It is interesting to note that the day we were there with NBC to film a segment on the haunted house, we too experienced paranormal activities as Pat Kosharek gave us a tour of the building. We started in the basement and in one of the small storage rooms we detected an energy anomaly that registered high on our EMF meter that detects electromagnetic fields.

This energy anomaly literally floated around within the room. Several times over the next few hours we returned to that same room and detected this irregularity. We took Polaroid pictures but alas no ghostly images appeared. We did pick up some weird vertical lines on one of the images taken in the basement room.

Pat Kosharek told us this was the room the Psychic had told her was haunted. It seems last Halloween night Pat Kosharek had invited students to spend the night in the haunted house and had invited a Psychic to attend with them.

We continued scanning all of the floors within

the building but the only other room that had registered paranormal activity was the office of Jeff R. Grundon, the Associate Director of Admissions. In his office we found a corner where a floor lamp was located gave off high energy readings. The energy anomaly that floated around the lamp area was continually moving about. We talked with Jeff and he says he can tell when Vera is present. It seems the hair on the back of his neck stands up when she is around.

Lamp in Jeff Grundon's office

Vera has played pranks on Jeff from time to time. Pranks such as pulling his door shut, even though there is a door stop that prevents the door from closing by itself. A box fan that will turn on by itself as he is looking at it. Other times he has noticed a foul odor erupt by his desk, even though his window was wide open at the time.

Lets look at some of the pranks that Vera has played on people. One time a part time security officer for the school, Mark Westlund, found the lights on in the building after he had made sure they were turned off. This happened on three consecutive Thursdays nights.

Westlund heard the soprano voice of a singer inside on the third Thursday night. He entered the hall and thought the singing was coming from the attic. He slowly climbed the stairs and checked the attic but no one was there. He then worked his way down, checking all of the rooms on the second and first floor. Nothing, but still the singing continued. The only thing left to check was the basement and that too was empty. Just as he was turning to leave he caught a faint glimpse of a whispy white figure at the end of the hall. Without further ado, he retreated from the house, double-time!

Dr. Donald Schwejda, a retired music professor claimed to have had his office door open and close without assistance. Professor Schwejda also heard footsteps in the hall when no one was there. The stories go on and on. The ghost is known to sing, play the piano, walk about the hall creating the sounds of footsteps, the rustle of a long dress is heard in a locked room, whispered voices and loud sighs, open and shut doors, turn on lights, frighten students, faculty and dogs.

Kristin Hofman, editor of the Pacific University Index, tells of her experience in meeting Vera for the first time. "I was in Knight Hall working upstairs with two other people. Before our very eyes we saw Vera turn on the box fan across the room. The fan was not on, and no one turned it on. Vera did it herself."

Kristin Hofman wrote "In 1979, two reporters of the Index, Lance Giles and Dan Grubb, stayed overnight in Knight Hall as part of a story they were writing for the Index on Vera. At 5:30 a.m. they left in fright. They reported hearing footsteps, hearing an alto voice singing, and the rustling of a long skirt on the ground. They also saw lights going off and on. One of the reporters played the piano, and twice heard a female voice scream in his ear 'Oh, please stop!' They immediately left the building."

Richard T. Read, Archivist/Curator of the Harvey W. Scott Memorial Library was very helpful and friendly. He has amassed a large collection of articles and newspaper clippings about Vera. Anyone interested in learning more about the resident ghost of Pacific University should contact him for information.

THE SPIRIT OF ELVIS PRESLEY

Elvis Presley

The Spirit of Elvis Presley lives on board his famous 'Elvis Presley TCB Tour Bus that is owned by Fantastic Museum of Redmond, Oregon. The authors were treated to a private tour of Elvis Presley's Tour Bus of 1976 by David Vetti, Director of Public Relations. During the two hours that the authors spent on the bus, amazing things happened!

First off, we were hoping to get a good story on the ghost of Elvis Presley which has been reported seen on this bus by various fans. We should state for the record that we were not big fans of Elvis Presley so we were not expecting to see or feel anything out of the ordinary. We had decided to stop for an interview since the Elvis Presley Bus was featured on the same segment of NBC Good Evening as our ghost story of Liberty Theater in Astoria, Oregon.

David Vetti, driver of the bus, was very outgoing and polite. He offered to show us the interior of the bus and to allow us to take pictures and perform EMF scans with our electronic equipment. The bus was at the repair shop for a check up prior to its journey back to Graceland for Elvis' 60th Birthday Gala. We were delighted to have been invited to tour the bus and to take a test ride on it.

David Vetti

As we stepped into the TCB bus, we were impressed with the open living room type of scene. The floor was carpeted with a well used red carpet with two large white initials, 'E P', interwoven in the carpet. Two blue chairs, the kind you would find in any living room, sat one across from the other. There was also a narrow blue couch against a wall of windows, normal and comfortable in every way. A table of Elvis memorabilia sat against the wall across the floor from the couch, and the room was definitely set up in tribute to the man who once traveled in this vehicle. Many pictures of Elvis hung around the room as a tribute to the King.

Hallway of the Elvis T.C.B. Bus

As we looked around, everything felt so normal, like going into a showroom and looking through the motorhomes on display. We departed from the repair shop for the test drive. We were amazed at how nice it rode on the highway. While we were cruising down Highway 97, Sharon was talking to the driver, David Vetti. I was walking down the corridor to the back bedroom using the EMF meter, scanning for sudden spikes in

Sharon Gill, inside the Elvis T.C.B. Bus

Prior to stepping onto the bus, David Vetti recounted some strange incidences that had occurred on the bus. In one incident, the lights on one of the berths had mysteriously turned on when no was around.

Well, as I was walking down the passage way toward the back bedroom, the EMF meter registered a strong reading at one of the lower berths. David Vetti confirmed that the berth I had registered high readings in was the same berth that had experienced the lights being turned on by themselves!

David Vetti, driver for the past two years, can honestly say he has never seen the ghost of Elvis but after talking to him for over two hours, he has felt the spirit of Elvis.

There is no doubt in our minds, after listening to Vetti describe his experiences conducting tours of the bus, he has been touched by the spirit of that great man whose bus he is now driving. There is something

Elvis Presley's Teddy Bear and Pricilla, his wife.

It appears to be an ordinary bus, but for some unexplained reason, the spirit of Elvis Presley is there. The previous driver, Glen Tadlock who had designed the T.C.B. (Taking Care of Business in a Flash) logo, told Vetti how difficult it was to not be the driver any longer. (Tadlock had purchased the bus and taken it on tour for several years.) Tadlock had a tear in his eye as he spoke of how attached and emotionally involved he had become to the bus and to Elvis Presley.

David Vetti spoke softly to us as he described his realization after two months of driving that he was somehow emotionally attached to the bus. Even as Vetti spoke, a tear formed in his eyes as he told us the type of person Elvis was and how he had loved everyone and cared for them. For whatever supernatural reason, the energy or substance that was Elvis can still be experienced in that bus today. That amazing and wonderful giving attitude of helping others permeates the interior of that bus. Many visitors to the bus have had a religious-like awakening as the spirit of Elvis moved upon them.

As we prepared to depart, Vetti told us that on occasions, when Elvis was in the mood, Tadlock would fire-up the bus around 3:00 A.M. so Elvis could drive, because Elvis really loved this bus.

Elvis drove it three or four times logging more than 350 miles behind the wheel. Elvis would drive from Graceland down local streets and as far as Mississippi.

Elvis did two tours with this coach and was in the process of preparing for his third tour when the King passed away. This Elvis T.C.B. coach toured with such names as Lacy J. Dalton, George Jones, Loretta Lynn's band, Lynn Anderson, Charlie Daniels band and the Oak Ridge Boys.

Yes, David Vetti may not have seen the ghost of Elvis himself, but he truly has felt the spirit of the 'King' and that influence has changed his life forever.

Elvis Presley T.C.B Tour Bus of 1976

The 'King'
January 8, 1935 to August 16, 1977

THE THIRSTY SPIRIT

Since I was six, I have moved five times. On the last move which was to West Hills, California, something a little weird happened. When we got to our new house, my sister and I did our share of "we probably won't make any friends!" Or "We'll probably get shot the first day we go to school!" Or "They'll regret this move, I know it!" But usually after a month we get used to the place and love it there, but I didn't know about any body else but I just had this feeling of being constantly watched.

I had asked my sister if she felt watched to, and she said, "Don't worry it should go away soon. It's probably because you're not used to the surroundings yet."

My sister had the top bunk in our room. I used to have the top bunk, but I fell out and moved a back bone out of place. Then I fell again the following night so we had to switch beds. One night I was having trouble sleeping. It was about 11:45 P.M. or so and everyone had gone to sleep. I was just thinking about the day that I had just had. When suddenly I distinctively heard a cup being placed down in the kitchen, as if someone had just gotten a drink. Then I heard the refrigerator door slam. I had thought everyone was asleep, so I said, "Sarah, did you hear that?" Sarah?"

"What?"

"Did you hear that?"

"No. Go to sleep!"

So I stayed in bed waiting to see if anyone was going to pass by, because all the rooms were on our side of the house, and if they went to one of their rooms I'd seem them. I stayed and waited for about five minutes, and no one came by. I got out of bed and went to the kitchen to see if whoever made the noise was still out there. There was no one out there and there was no cup on the counter or in the sink.

RED HEART TEDDY BEAR

While I was growing up, wait, I am still growing up, well when I was about six my mother gave me a teddy bear she had made on her sewing machine. It was all red with little white hearts all over it. My mother never put any eyes on (maybe because I would probably tear them off) so I would just imagine them on. I wasn't too bright on finding great names for my stuffed animals. So I just thought, well hey, it's red and it has hearts all over it so I'll call it "Red Hearts" and that is how it got it name.

Carolina Oester and her Red Teddy Bear

Well you could say that the bear had a rough beating. I'm now thirteen and have had to sew up the bear nine times, but it's still my favorite thing! Every night I'd have Red Hearts on my bed with me so I'd have something to cuddle up to in case I got scared or had a nightmare, it was my own little personal shrink. I didn't really expect it to answer me, but I'd just tell Red Hearts my feelings, so I wouldn't keep it all bottled up inside.

The weirdest thing that did happen was with my mentioned earlier teddy bear, Red Hearts. My sister and my brother (who slept in the next two rooms) said that I had started singing hand clapping game songs in the middle of the night or I would start crying in my sleep. My sister said sometimes I'd even start carrying on a conversation with someone. It started becoming every night that this might happen. Until one night I didn't have Red Hearts by my side, he was all dirty so I put him in the wash. Nothing happened. And of course I just thought they were trying to scare me.

Previously my brother David had hid a voice-activated tape recorder in shelves that were on my bed. Sure enough, the tape recorder had recorded some-thing. But a very peculiar thing happened when my brother played the tape back for me. Occasionally there would be like a whipping noise or there would be like a static kind of noise. One part of the tape there was a weird noise then the tape snapped.

My brother and I wanted to hear what had hap-pened next, so he taped the broken tape back together but we couldn't hear what that noise exactly was after all that. I do not feel that my teddy bear was trying to hurt me but he is trying to be a friend to me during a time when I felt like I needed a friend.

Authors Note:

It is not uncommon for a tape recorder to pickup ghostly voices or noises. This is commonly referred as the 'Electronic Voice Phenomenon' or 'EVP'.

AWAKENED BY A SHADOW

I was about twelve years of age when this happened to me. We were living on Stonehenge Lane in Ft. Walton Beach, Florida. I had gone to bed for the evening and was fast asleep. As was the custom, we always left a light on in the hallway so we would not be afraid of the dark. I remember laying in bed and seeing a dim light shining into the doorway because my bed was facing that light.

Suddenly, I awakened from my sleep. I could see a shadow standing at the foot of my bed. The apparition that stood before the bed was a dark image. I could see a definite figure standing at the foot of my bed, with the light behind it, outlining the form of a man.

The figure was short in stature with arms to the side, just standing in front of me. I remember lying there for a second or two, just staring at this figure. I finally lifted myself up unto my elbows, fixated upon this figure standing in front of me. The thought came to me, that this is my dad because he was short.

However looking back on this, I realize that the shadowy outline of a person was too small to be my dad. I said, "Oh Dad, you scared the 'sh*t' out of me!" I remember thinking clearly in that split second that I'm in trouble for cussing. I think this is why this event is so vivid in my mind. The cuss word and the fear of getting into trouble with my dad were burned deep into my mind.

After my remark the figure disappeared. It wasn't an ordinary now you're here and now you're gone like in a magic trick or a scene from 'I Dream of Jennie' types of disappearance.

AWAKENED BY A SHADOW-- THE MOTHER

Well, to begin with, Sixteen years ago I was living on Stonehenge Lane in Ft. Walton Beach, Florida. I was having some emotional turmoil in my life then and totally disregarded the strange things I had observed, thinking I was losing it. Now, sixteen years later, my daughter and her husband were visiting us from New York. We were talking about us writing a book on ghost stories and my daughter told us about being awakened by a shadow. This is the mother's side of the story.

One day, while living on Stonehenge, I was walking from the family room through the dining room into the kitchen. I caught a glimpse of a shadow of a man in the living room. I stood and looked at the shadow for a minute until the shadow of the man vanished from view. I was home alone. I was scared to death. I told myself that I was just seeing things and that there was nothing there. I had convinced myself that because of the stress I was under, I imagined a shadow of a man.

Imagine my relief, when sixteen years later, I discovered that I was not the only one to have seen that shadow of a man. My daughter had seen the same ghostly image as I had observed so many years ago. Who or what that image of a man represented, I do not know. But I can tell you how relieved I was to know someone else had the same experience. I never related my ghostly vision to anyone for fear of being called crazy.

THE CLOSET GHOST

Once a person lives in a house for years, the noises associated with that house become known. Hi, my name is Sarah, this is one of my experiences that happened while living in Los Angeles. I knew my house very well, at least its noises. I knew who was walking across the living room by the creaks and groans of the floor. I knew which boards were squeaky in the hall. I knew the sound of family members moving about in their rooms. All my family members living in the house knew the sounds of the other persons.

The house had a raised foundation. It was nearly two feet off the ground. All the houses in our development were constructed that way. The raised foundation created a chamber effect that clearly vibrated the sounds of movement. I never liked the house. The house always seemed oppressive. It wasn't ugly and it wasn't pretty. It just had, what my friends and I called, "bad vibes".

That house made noises it shouldn't have made sometimes. For example, the house made sounds like my stepfather walking across the living room to the refrigerator, when he was away on business trips or in the same room with us. Sometimes at night it sounded like my stepfather was walking across the floor at night, but the door to my parents room never opened. My younger sister, Carrie, swore that she saw someone walking pass our room and then the kitchen door opened and closed.

A particular experience really rattled me. It was in February of 1994. I was still out of school due to the Northridge Earthquake in January. Carrie was babysitting and my brother was working so I was home alone. I was reading a book in the living room sitting with my back to the wall. Behind the wall was my parent's closet.

Sarah Oester with her book

As I read, I heard the door to the closet open and the clothes being moved in my parent's bedroom. I listened to the clothes moving for another couple of minutes before I got up to see what was happening. I walked into my parent's room to see what it was. The closet door was open and the room temperature was about twenty degrees colder then the rest of the house. I decided that whatever was in there, since it wasn't destructive, could exist without me interfering. I left the room and went back to reading.

HAUNTED HOLLYWOOD MANSION

This story comes from a gentleman living in Scappoose, Oregon, seven miles south of St.Helens and takes place in Hollywood, California.

The property located in Hollywood, beyond Brea Terrace, in downtown Hollywood. The two houses were built back in 1909 were located n the side of a hill. The big house was like 7,000 square feet with an Olympic size swimming pool. The older, smaller house, used as a guest house and for partying. This was the house I stayed in for a time. The house, owned once by the Broadway Producer Mark Hellinger and his wife Gladys. Gladys did not want the older guest house torn down. She loved that old house.

The house was bought by Gail Patrick Jackson, the movie star and her husband Cornwell Jackson, who was an agent for one of the big time movie companies. They bought the property and moved into the big house and kept the guest house for guests.

During their business they eventually came around to producing the Perry Mason series. It became a house in which Erle Stanley Gardner would stay when he was there going over scripts and this kind of things. They had experiences in that house similar to mine.

When I moved into the completely furnished house, I kept all the bedroom things but moved out the living room things and moved my own things in there.

I was checking light switches to see that things worked. Everything worked but none of the plug-in lamps would work in the living room. So I got several long extension cords and plugged them in extra outlets in the upstairs bedroom and ran the cords down the stairs into the living room. I went down to the main house and asked them to please call an electrician sometime and find out why, I can't get any of the floor outlets to work in the living room.

A few days go by and every time I'd walk into the room I'd have to manually turn the lights on. Several days later, the electrician arrived and could find nothing wrong with the floor outlets. He flipped the main switch behind the door and all of the outlets were working. All the lamps plugged into the floor outlet came on just the way they should.

I had flipped that main switch a million times with nothing happening in the living room. I thought perhaps the switch was for the chandelier.

About a month or so later I cam home very late and went into my carpeted walk-in closet to undress and get into my pajamas. I took my pants and hung them up. When I did, all my change fell on the floor. I thought, to heck with it, it's too late. I'd pick up the change the next morning.

I have a miniature toy-poodle dog, named 'Bambi' and she was always a very quiet dog, she never yapped but she was always right there. She would sleep on the bed next to me. The dog was somewhat restless that night but I felt it was because I'd been out late or something. I didn't really think anything about it.

When I woke up the next morning, all the change I had on the closet floor was stacked neatly in pennies, nickels, dimes and quarters on the night table. I thought, "Did I sleep walk, or pick up my change or what did I do?"

I tried to retrace my memory of what I did and what I didn't do. None of it made sense, I thought well, I must have picked up the change. But I would not have neatly stacked the change. I would have thrown it on the dresser or the night table.

I worked out of the house for my business and used the sun room a lot. It was just great as I had set the sun room up as an office. Many times, I'd be sitting there and I'd hear someone downstairs saying,

"Russell . . . Russell."

I would wonder who in the world was there. I hadn't seen anyone coming up the 32-step stairs from the motor court which was the only way someone could enter the house.

I would go to the landing at the head of the stairs and yell down, "Who's there?"

There would be no response and I'd go downstairs and search the house. Not a soul would be there and this happened frequently during the year and a half that I stayed in that house. Then while downstairs searching, I would hear footsteps from someone walking around upstairs and I'd hear them call my name.

I had a lady friend who was mystic or something. She was a German lady, tested by a European organization for psychic abilities. She could tell you by looking at a glass of water and by touching it, what minerals are in it. She worked with the Los Angeles Police Department on finding lost children.

One day she came up to the house and after walking around in the upstairs portion of the house, declared "Oh, you have a ghost up here."

I asked her, "how do you know I have a ghost?" I had told her nothing of my experiences that had occurred in this house.

She said, "Well, she is standing right there!"

I said, "I don't see anything."

She said, "She's here!"

I said, "Well, that accounts for some mysterious things going on in the house. Since she is friendly, who cares."

One day, I went downstairs and got in my car. It was a hot day and I didn't want to take my dog. I knew I'd be out of the car quite a while so I left her at home. I left the house all open and I left the front door open with only the big heavy wooden screen door shut. The screen door did not have a latch, so when I left, I took the large fiber mat and propped it up against the door. My little toy dog weighed about four pounds.

I went and did my errands and when I came back suddenly, the lady who owned the large house stuck her head out her upstairs dressing room window, which faced the front door of the guest house. She hollered out, "Russ, come over here, I need to talk to you."

I said, "Okay."

I walked down to the main house. She said, "I wish you'd take better care of your dog. You know how these people are. They come up to the motor court driving 90-miles an hour, because it's a winding driveway. They don't even look where they're going. I was getting very worried about your dog."

I said, "What is wrong with my dog?"

She said, "Well, I heard the screen door slam so I looked out the window and saw 'Bambi' coming down the stairs. I went back to putting on my makeup when I again looked out the window. This time your dog was sunning herself on the motor court. I worried because she is black and the blacktop street is black and someone might not see her if they pulled in to the motor court driving fast. Then a few minutes later, she got up and walked up the steps and I heard the screen door slam shut."

I left the house and went up the 32-steps to my front door. There was the fiber mat propped up against the screen door. My dog was in the house. I called her up on the phone and said, "I think there is something going on here that you're not aware of. Bambi is in this house, I propped the screen door purposely with this mat so she couldn't get out."

She answered, "Oh, then you found Gladys."

I said, "Gladys who?"

That was when she told me the story about Gladys and Mark Hellinger. Everyone who has stayed in that house has had some ghost experience. She said, "Are you frightened by it?"

I said, "I think it is interesting."

So from that point on, I became more alert to things. One day I had a friend call up and say he had a buddy who was coming in from Connecticut or someplace, would I mind a house guest for a couple of days because he was on his way to someplace else.

My house guest had brought his TV set with him, which was all he brought with him. He asked me if I had a TV set in the other bedroom and I said no but he was welcome to bring his along for his bedroom. He arrived. Every night he'd go into his room and shut his door and I would shut my door. There is a hall between the two bedrooms.

One night, I awakened by somebody or something shaking me. It was about 1:00 or 1:30 in the morning. I was thinking what is all this about. Knowing about this ghost thing, I thought maybe I ought to wake up, so I did, I sat on the edge of the bed and now my dog's sitting, ears perking and looking around, like something is going on.

I put on my bathrobe and opened the door. I looked across the hall and I could see the flickering of the TV lights. So I went over to my house guest's door and I started to knock on it and I thought, no, if he's asleep I'll wake him up. He's got the TV on so what is the big deal. I listened at the door and I didn't hear anything except the TV. I thought, well, everything OK, so then I went back to bed and went back to sleep.

The next morning down in the kitchen he said, "Thanks for waking me up. I owe you a blanket and a sheet because I burned a hole in the blanket and the sheet with a cigarette."

He said, "I awoke up about midnight and could not get back to sleep so I turned on the TV to watch the news or something. I normally don't smoke in bed.

Forgive me but I'm glad you woke me up at 1:15 because I probably would have set the house on fire."

I said, "I did not wake you up, I had walked to your door but decided not to enter your room to wake you."

He said, "Well, somebody woke me up!"

I said, "Oh, it probably was Gladys, she didn't want to have her damn house burned down."

He said, "You're kidding me, there is a ghost in this house?"

He was here about a week, but every night he propped a chair against the door knob, to keep her out of his room. He decided to depart earlier then he had originally planned, saying he had unfinished business elsewhere. I smiled.

AS I TOUCHED THE WALL

Well, I should start at the beginning. I was a young eighteen year old, not quite immature but still had lots of roads to travel before I matured. My company had just been through one vicious firefight. I was out on the perimeter, way out as it turns out and did not know the full status of the command base.

The perimeter moved, in several steps, closer to the base by a mile. I was unaware of this move. In the battle, my radio and ammo bearer became lost. Stunned and numb from the action and the resulting silence added to the strangeness of the night.

I began to think again since during the battle I don't believe I was aware of my actions. Since there was no breeze, the smell of the battle hung in the air. I flipped down the night-vision and scanned the area. I saw a concentrated group of movement but could not make out any distinct shapes. Not wanting to fire on 'friendlies' I just sat and watched. I remember the silence more than anything, and the weird green haze that the night-vision gave to everything.

As I watched, some movement began to approach and take shape. This was someone that I knew but not very well. He had tears in his eyes and a quiver to his voice when he said "Hey" (A common hello for the times) that caused me to ask what was wrong. He began to tell me how he was going to miss his family and how sad they would be.

I guess I was still numb because I did not catch on to what was happening. I had a brief conversation with him and several others that night. I ran through all the emotions I was capable of feeling. I never questioned what was happening. Each individual was very different. I made a promise that night and I just finished keeping the last of them. I now feel free to share what I have been carrying around for twenty-five years.

Each individual I talked to that night died in the battle. The promises I made that night ranged from saying goodbye to much more personal pledges. As I completed each promise I experienced a host of things, from mystery pats on the back to the feeling of intense warmth. It's over now, but I have one more task to complete, this one is for me. There is a certain wall I have to visit and say my goodbyes.

I made the trip to the wall. I didn't know what to expect, but just felt the need to make the trip. To close a chapter of my life, to say goodbye to something I lived with for so long, to end the dreams, and to live for my future, it all seemed worth it. As I approached the wall I felt nothing. I stopped several paces from the wall and took a deep breath. I ran through the names again and decided to visit them in the same order as when completing their last requests.

I went to the first of the names. It took me some time to find it but I eventually was standing, slightly bent, looking at the name. Like I said, I didn't know what to expect and surprised that I felt nothing. Then I reached out and touched the name. I felt the same emotions I experienced more than twenty-five years ago when I started on this task, followed by the intense warmth I felt when I completed his request. I stepped away from the wall. I wasn't sure I could take five more of these experiences in one day.

As I stepped up to the next name and touched the wall, the replay of emotions was the same as in the past, but it was if the intensity decreased. Maybe I could finish this after all. I went through the next three names in the same fashion. Tired and a bit drained so I turned away from the wall to find a place to sit. I took one step and heard a familiar voice say "Hey." I was snapped alert by this response. I turned back and somehow was directly in front of the last of the names.

Ironically, the first individual I had encountered

so long ago was the last request I had completed, and the most intense. For whatever reason, the intensity was not there. I experienced, as I touched the wall for the last time, a feeling of completion, relief, or whatever it is you feel when you have done something good.

I walked away from the wall that day with tears streaming down my face but, with a good feeling. I'm not sure I'll ever return. I don't think I'll need to.

Authors Note:
The Vietnam Memorial Wall is in Washington, D.C., next to the Lincoln Memorial. This Wall has touched many Vietnam Veterans over the years and truly was necessary to help those of us who served in that time of conflict and lost friends and comrades in battle.

GHOST IN MAINE

I love ghost stories. I have had some really wild things happen to me when I was a kid, here is one such story. First, let me give you the background of the house that this took place in. This house built in the late 1700's is a farmhouse with a barn attached to the house. In 1975 the house had a fire and burned down, along with many memories.

The house was a Summer place for my family. The house has been in my family for sixty-seven years. My grandfather originally paid $2,500.00 for the house and five acres of land.

My first story that I heard was about a spirit that came walking past my parent's bed about 3:00 in the morning. The story goes like this. The year was 1963 and I was just one year old, the family including my grandmother was there getting the place ready to close for the winter.

It was about 3:00 in the morning and everyone was in bed sound asleep. All of a sudden, my Mom woke up and thought she heard one of us kids going by her bed to the bathroom, which was downstairs but you could use the back stairs to get there. She woke my Father up to get the flashlight, so that whoever it was wouldn't trip. When my father shown the light in the path that he heard the foot steps there were nothing there.

He got up and checked on all of us, we were all asleep. He went back to the bedroom and shined the flashlight on the floor and could see foot prints on the floor, the foot prints led to the attic. My Father didn't bother going any further so he turned around and went back to bed. The next day the foot prints were still there. My Father could plainly see they were a child's foot prints. Years later, we found out a five year old child suffocated in the attic.

GRANDFATHERS LAST SUIT

I don't believe in ghosts. I have been in the following situation: I was taken hostage and trussed up
in the back of a car by three persons. I expected to be
killed. I would have expected to have had some sort of
telepathic link to my nearest and dearest, but I didn't.
I am a skeptic but . . .

My wife and I had been fortunate enough to move
into my grandparent's house when they had moved into
a nursing home. My Grandmother died, but my Grandfather stayed alert and active for years, although he
gradually declined. He had several bouts of pneumo-
nia, but still stayed alert and active.

We needed more room to store my wife's and my
stuff so we moved all of Grandfathers' things into la-
beled boxes and stored upstairs in the closet on the
top shelf. We could immediately get anything he wanted
from the closet. He had no trouble remembering where
things were, either. But eventually, well past ninety
years of age, my Grandfather died. His funeral planned,
my mother retrieved a suit in which to bury his body
in. But . . .

I taught at a community college then, and had
just gotten home. I went upstairs to go to the bathroom. As I got to the head of the stairs, and looked
into the bathroom, I saw the mirrored door of the medi-
cine chest on the bathroom wall slowly swing open.
My hair rose. This door has a latch on it to prevent it
from opening by accident. Then I heard a creak and
looked to the left, and the door of the closet where I
kept my clothes slowly swung open.

OK, fine, I admit that this door had an old-fashioned latch and didn't work all that well. Still, this had
never happened before. I gritted my teeth and walked
forward and shut first the closet door, then the medi-
cine chest door. No cold chills, no spooky lights or

noises, nothing. But . . .

A few days later my wife asked where one of my gray pair of pants had gone. I still don't know. I've never seen them again, and bought another pair to match the suit coat. Was Gandfather wearing them? I don't know. It was a closed casket service, and I didn't ask to see. I guess I didn't want to know, but my mother thinks, and I'd tend to agree, that Grandpa, who was always a snappy dresser, didn't care for her choice of suit pants. The day I had my weird experience was the day he was prepared for his burial.

I've never seen those pants again. Who knows? I don't, but ever since then I've been a lot more tolerant toward the paranormal, and will be . . . until someone can find that pair of pants!

FLOATING COFFEE CUP

I was at work one day and talking to my co-worker, Frank. About eight steps away to my right was a doorway with no door which led to a storage area and bathroom. There were no other doors leading in or out of the storage area. It was in the middle of the afternoon, probably about 2:00 P.M. or so.

As I stood talking with Frank, I saw a coffee cup float across the doorway. The coffee cup acted as if it was being hung by one finger through the handle. The coffee cup floated from left to right and about chest height. I saw this out of the corner of my eye. The handle was to the left.

My heart missed a beat as I thought to myself "nahh!" I was about to continue talking when Frank said, "did you see that?" So I guess I wasn't alone. We marched right back to the doorway, into the well-lit room and looked. No coffee cup anywhere. Nothing and that was that.

HAUNTED PIT TOILET

My wife and I were bicycling in Maine, headed for Bucksport as our next stop. We stopped at a roadside rest for lunch near Bucksport. There was a pit toilet about fifty steps away from the table we had selected, so I went off to use it. I hadn't been inside more than ten seconds when the whole thing started rocking just as if someone was doing it from the outside. (My wife does have that kind of sense of humor.)

So I yelled, "Cut that out, dear!" And it stopped right away. I had 'done my duty' and so jumped right out to catch her. To my amazement, there she was, back at the table way off yonder! I looked at the Outhouse and tried to rock it. It was mounted solidly on a cement foundation and I could not budge it. I went back to the table and said nothing. It was obvious that she had never left the table. Then it was her turn to use the pit toilet. When she returned she said, "I thought that you had followed me!"

"Why, what happened?", I asked.

"Well, I was inside using it and someone started pounding on the walls. It was on all four sides like someone was running around it. Are you sure it wasn't you?" She asked, readying her water bottle for a squirt. I convinced her that it wasn't me and told her 'my' story, too. Much the same thing. She also added that she yelled "Cut it out sweetie!" And then it stopped immediately. I surely wish that we had stopped the lady who used it after we did. I wonder if anything unusual happened while she was inside but I just didn't have the nerve.

Later, when we got to Bucksport, we told our friend who lives there about what we experienced. He told us that he had heard stories that the place was haunted and that motorists passing by sometimes reported seeing a 'leg' sticking out of the ground.

POSSESSIVE GHOST

This is a story that my wife, Cindy, told me about a house she visited. About ten years ago Cindy went to visit four male friends who shared a house that was haunted. This particular ghost was a female who manifested herself by doing housework and such. An old-fashioned ghost, I guess. Her friends had told her about this ghost, and she had noticed things like dishes getting washed and clothes folded and put away.

Ever the skeptic, she thought her buddies were playing a joke on her by doing these things and then saying the ghost did it. Until one afternoon all four of her male friends went out, leaving Cindy alone in the house with the ghost. Seeing the house in a mess, and never one to let the hired help do all the work, Cindy started to wash the dishes.

First, a glass she was putting down after washing it fell. Then a plate she had put down minutes before, fell. A little spooky, but easily explained by chance. But, as you can guess, other things started to fall, and eventually cabinet doors began to slam shut behind her. As the kitchen began to erupt into chaos, my wife realized that she was being harassed by a jealous woman!

A ghost who was jealous of her 'men'. She immediately said in a loud voice, "I'm only visiting, and I'm not going to take them away from you." All the violence ceased, and my wife's stay was pretty uneventful after that. Of course, when she found dishes put away or laundry washed, she didn't think it was a practical joke anymore.

POSSESSED ELECTRONICS

About two years ago while I was working for a Photography company as a photographer, we had to shoot a composite picture of a sorority in a local park. We took portraits using the natural background. When we take portraits, we use video proofing which allows the subject to choose which picture to order without seeing the real proofs.

Anyway, we set up all the video equipment which consisted of the following: A portable generator, a grabber (it grabs a picture at a time, and shows it on a monitor that is divided into quarters, and also saves the pictures on a floppy), a monitor, the camera, and a thermal printer for printing out pictures.

When we turned on the equipment, the silhouette of a person appeared on the monitor. This was strange because the picture used the entire monitor screen which should show four pictures. The grabber separates the picture into four segments by two perpendicular lines, and had no features which allowed it to show a complete undivided picture.

Anyway, I got a printout of the silhouette, and I think I still have it at home if it didn't get lost in the move. We were pressed for time and were trying to get the equipment functional. We tried resetting each piece of equipment (on/off/reset buttons) but that didn't do it, so we unplugged each piece one by one. No luck. Next we turned off the generator, unplugged everything completely and started over from scratch. This time everything functioned properly.

THE UNFAITHFUL WIFE

My aunt and uncle purchased a house about fifteen years ago. The house was really large with eight rooms and sold for a very low price due to the fact that a very gruesome murder took place there.

The Real Estate Agent told a story of a man and his wife who had owned the house previously. This woman was unfaithful and her husband found out so he planned on killing them both. He told his wife he was leaving on a fishing trip for the weekend, knowing full well, she would take advantage of the situation. He went to a local bar for about two hours, and returned home to find a strange car in the driveway.

The husband entered the house with a gun in his hand, went into the bedroom and found his wife and her lover in bed together. He shot both of them and then after contemplating what he had done and the consequences, he put the gun to his own head and shot himself.

My aunt and uncle thought "so what! It's a beautiful house at a great price, so what if some people died in here." Boy, were they mistaken! Two days later during the night they were awakened by three loud voices arguing. "You unfaithful b**ch" and "Put the gun down Harold, you could hurt someone with that thing!"

Then four gunshots rang out and a very maniacal laugh was heard five minutes later. You could hear, "Why did I do it?" The final shot was heard thirty seconds later.

The final moments in these peoples lives had been reenacted for one last time. This reenactment would occur every two weeks and was a very regular occurrence. My aunt and uncle decided to stay up late on that one evening to investigate the matter.

At approximately 1:30 a.m., my aunt told me that even though all the doors and windows were shut, a strong wind swept thought the house, they saw nothing but felt a definite presence. Then they heard the arguing, but before the shots rang out, my aunt told the ghost "Harold, why don't you lay the gun down. You can divorce her, you'll get the house, the cars, everything."

It was still for a moment and then they heard, "Hey, you know you're probably right, I want a divorce, you unfaithful b**ch. I'm going to bleed you dry!" Footsteps were heard walking down the stairs, the front door opened and slammed shut. After that night, the voices and gunshots were never heard again. My aunt and uncle have never had any more problems living in that beautiful large home.

THE ALGEBRA BOOK GHOST

My house was built in 1927 and five years ago, the family living next to our house was murdered by the father who then killed himself. Now this happens in a different house but it is very similar and looks like my home. When that house burned down, the owner of my house bought the lot to expand the property of the existing home.

The first week we moved in little things happened such as my picnic dishes and cheese grater disappeared. The dishes have since shown up but the grater is still missing. My husband chalks this up to my forgetfulness which isn't true.

Then one day my husband was unpacking stuff in the basement and when it got to be late, he decided to retire for the night. He came upstairs and went to bed, the next morning he went down stairs to finish and found an old broom at the bottom of the stairs. No one had placed that old broom at the bottom of the stairs! It was not there when he was unpacking the boxes. He checked with the neighbors but none had lost an old broom. This was when I started wondering about a ghost.

My husband, a nonbeliever, said I was nuts and that ghosts don't exist! But things continued to happen. Child-like footsteps were heard upstairs in the hall. Especially when we put our children to bed. Our son was sleeping in a crib and our daughter would fall asleep in our bedroom.

One time we heard the footsteps while we were walking up the stairs and could see the hallway. There was no one in the hall, but we could hear the footsteps. I finally solved the running footsteps by yelling up the stairs, "It's time for bed and I do not want to hear any more running around." It stopped and has never happened again.

One day I came home from work and went to the kitchen to start cooking dinner. I got stuff out of the cabinets and opened the oven door. Immediately, all of this heat escaped from the oven. I looked at the knobs on the stove, the oven was turned to OFF. I was very upset because by this time, strange things were happening at least once a week. I got mad, really mad, I started to yell that they were not allowed to touch anything in the kitchen. I did not want them to burn down the house. I then proceeded to turn on two stove burners to LOW and then bent down to pick up the pots to place on the two burners. When I placed the two pots on the burners, I noticed the stove had been turned from LOW to MED-HIGH! I lost it, I warned the ghost that it was to leave it alone. It has never happened again.

I have heard a voice that said it needed to get its algebra done and I responded that it need not worry about it now. I have only heard it once or twice and it has been a good year since the last time I heard it. My neighbors called me one day this past summer and asked if we were having any more happenings lately. I said not too much and why did she ask? She said, "I saw something that really freaked me out and I wanted to tell you about it.

She said that she looked outside her window and saw her son on a tree swing. When he got bored with swinging, he climbed off and the swing slowly came to a dead stop. Suddenly, the swing started to twirl back and forth like maybe a child was twisting it but on one was on it. It was calm day with no wind. She went outside and stopped the swing because it gave her chills.

We have had our share of unusual things happening but to this day, I can't get my husband to admit that we do or had a ghost in our house. A year ago, he admitted it to his mother but never once to me. We have had our house blessed three months after buying it and the things stopped for about four months but then they started again but not as bad as the first few months.

Like I said, we get something that happens in the house every once in a while. Just to remind us that something is still here. I believe it is the youngest child and the oldest child or mother.

The reasoning for this is that not too long ago, my son's toys started to play all by themselves until I said I am watching this show and would you please stop that. It has not happened again. That house was located in upstate New York.

SHADOWY APPARITION

When I was a young boy, I had a friend who called me and my family over to their home late one night. My friend saw something and was very frightened. When we arrived at her home, she showed us to the wall in her living room. On the wall, there was a shadow of a sort-of bat.

She explained to us that she tried to remove the shadow with soap and water but was unable to. We

went to the couch to talk to her. As we talked, I observed the bat growing with the horns of the bat eventually stretching across the ceiling. The bat eventually
disappeared before we departed and never returned!

THE PET PIG

When I was young, my aunt told me a story of
her best friend's pet pig. She had heard the story and
refused to believe it until she spent the night in her
friend's home. She witnessed the events for herself.
Apparently her friend had a pet pig that she kept in
the house for years.

Usually, the pig spent nights in the bathroom
with the door shut, because if they didn't keep the bathroom door closed, the pig would run into their bedroom and jump on the bed to sleep with them at night.

Years later, after the pig died, the couple would
hear the pet pig footsteps at night and feel the pet pig
jump on the bed! When they would turn on the lights,
they would see nothing. The only time they didn't hear
or feel the pig was on the nights they closed the bathroom door.

NEW ZEALAND EXPERIENCE

The following experiences happened to me when I was fifteen or sixteen. It was during the Easter period and I had gone to a youth camp. One night I sat on the couch talking to a friend for an extended period of time. I then had decided to wander over to join some other friends. To do this, I had to cross the main grass area and pass under some trees into the carpark (parking lot) where my friends were.

As I made my way to the trees, I was struck with an overwhelming feeling of danger. I suddenly knew that one of the trees contained something evil and that if I went near it, then it would harm me in some way. The weirdest thing about the whole incident was that I could and still could show you exactly where this took place. I remember getting the impression of something small and black sitting on a certain branch.

After several hours when I was finally able to calm down the camp caretakers told me a little about the area. Apparently, it was a battle site from early Maori wars and they have had several problems of entities staying around the area.

THE PREACHER'S GHOST

Here is a little story that my aunt swears to be true from my home state of Georgia. My aunt and her family used to be neighbors to a preacher and his family. Like so many of us they are all very devout Christians and the one time I personally met the preacher, I could tell right away that he was as good a person as any around. My aunt was very involved in the preacher's church and was usually the first one to the meetings, the choir, etc. This led to their involvement in the worst tragedies in the history of the area.

One day my Aunt, uncle and their two daughters were the first to arrive at choir practice as usual. The preacher was no where in sight though his car was parked outside the church. My cousins went looking for the preacher. The younger of the two, age seven at the time, found the preacher lying on the floor in his office. She thought he was sleeping and tried to awaken him but when she turned him over she found him to be dead with gunshot wounds. She ran to her parents and my Uncle in desperation. They tried some first aid and CPR but it was too late.

What had happened was the preacher had walked into his office to discover an armed man trying to rob the church of the last Sundays offerings. A struggle ensued and the preacher was killed. For the record his killer was caught and I believe is still waiting to be fried in a Georgia electric chair.

The day of the preacher's funeral, the entire community came out to support the widow and her family. While there were several dozen people in the house, the preacher's youngest daughter, age five, went outside to the back porch to be alone. A few minutes later she came back in the house and told her mother not to cry that it was okay. The mother then hugged the brave little girl and asked her where she had been. The little girl then told her mom that she had just talked to her daddy on the back porch and he had said that all would be well and that he would see them later.

GHOST IN THE HOUSE

About a year ago my uncle died, without leaving any type of a will. My father and his sister had to go to Miami to get his estate in order, and figure out what to do with his belongings. Anyway, my father ended bringing home my uncle's car and a big screen Sony television set.

The television set was almost brand new, and the person that found my uncle said that my uncle died while watching a football game and drinking a beer. This story made me feel kind of strange about the television set, but I soon forgot the story behind it. About a month after we started using the television set, I began noticing that it would turn off sometimes when I left the room to get something to eat. This only happened when nobody else was at home. Finally, about a month ago, it happened to my mom while she was watching it. About a week after that, it starting turning itself off right in front of our eyes.

A few days ago I noticed that somebody was recording a movie on the VCR underneath the television set. It was a movie that nobody in the house even liked or wanted to record. I looked at the VCR, and someone had actually set it to record this movie. Someone didn't hit the one touch recording button by accident. My mother has also awakened in the middle of the night to find the light in the television room on, and she clearly remembers turning the light off before we went to bed.

Yesterday, I turned the light on in that room, went outside for a few minutes and came back to the room only to find the lights turned off again. I was the only person home at the time. Last night, I remember leaving our gate unlocked so our parents could get in when they got home, and I heard somebody lock it. We have one of those security lights near the gate, the kind of one that comes on when someone walks under it. I ran outside the house when I heard the 'click' of the lock, the motion light wasn't on, and the gate was padlocked shut. I stared at the lock for a few seconds and felt very uneasy.

THE TIM-TIM GHOST

My twenty month old daughter and I had just moved out of my folks house where we had been staying since my divorce. I rented a one bedroom apartment on the ground level of a restored Victorian house of the late 1880's vintage. Two days after moving in I cleaned up the living room, putting my daughters toys in a laundry basket in the corner. The laundry basket was not full so nothing could have fallen out. I checked on my napping daughter in the bedroom which is at the far side of the kitchen. Then I proceeded to wash some dishes.

About five minutes later, I went into the living room and found two Fisher Price infant toys and a round beach ball scattered around the room. I checked on my daughter to find she was still fast asleep. My coming into the room awoke her. I sat on the bed talking to her. I heard a noise and looked back toward the kitchen to find the beach ball bouncing on the floor between the living room and kitchen. My daughter heard the sound of the bouncing ball coming from the living room and cried, "Tim-Tim" and got down off the bed and ran to the living room. I grabbed her and stayed the night with a friend.

About three weeks later, four days after Christmas, I was mopping the hallway and my daughter was again sleeping in her room. It was the same time of day as the previous experience. I saw a child run behind me toward the hallway. I ran to catch my daughter before she hit the freshly mopped area and perhaps hurt herself on the slippery floor. No one was there! My daughter was still sleeping in her bed. We spent that night at grandma's house.

New Years day, I was watching a television program and heard my daughter babbling away as she sometimes does to her dolls and to her Barney. It was again at the same time of day as the two previous experiences took place. My daughter should have been napping, so I went in to the bedroom to put her back to sleep. She was on the edge of her bed, swinging her feet and talking to the wall. She said, "Oh, Mama! It's Tim-Tim! Say hi Tim-Tim!"

We finally bought our first home which was eight years old and it looked normal, nothing spooky. On my birthday, my daughter who is now two years three months of age, gave me a birthday card that my husband helped her make. Below her name was written 'Tim-Tim'. I asked my husband, who knew nothing about this, why he had written the second name. He responded that my daughter had asked him to write that name.

Four months later, we went to visit my sister and her new baby at their home. When we arrived at their home and had gone inside, my daughter immediately said, "Tim-Tim, Come see the pretty Baby!" I freaked out!

HOSPITAL GHOST

Here is a ghost story that happened to me about four years ago while I was working for Mid-Michigan Regional Medical Center, a major hospital in Mid-Michigan. I was the midnight Computer Operator in the Computer room located in the basement. I have worked midnights for the past six years. I am wide awake during my shift and walking around when this happened to me.

I had been told that our computer room was haunted by the ghost of an old OR Nurse named Edith. It seems our computer room was at one time an OR (Operating Room). Well, Edith had a sense of humor as she would throw tape rings onto the floor unless you asked her not to do it. These tape rings are the plastic rings that go around the reel tapes that prevent them from unwinding all over the place.

This particular evening I sat in the Operations Office (Op's Office) which had a large window where you could see directly into the Computer Room itself. The Computer Room was a step up from the Op's Office and through a door to keep the climate controlled.

It was about 2:00 A.M. when I noticed that one of the Genicom printers had failed. I got up when I realized that the far Genicom had jammed again. These are 4-color dot matrix impact printers. They seem to jam constantly. I walked down that aisle and had to step over the tape ring that had fallen off a drive controller that was pretty much vibration free. Of course, to move that ring off of that drive would take an earthquake anyway. I was more then a little frustrated at the Genicom printers so I said, "Edith, that's not funny!" I then went to clear the jam. On my way back, the ring was back on the top of the drive controller!

It wouldn't have bothered me nearly as much if I hadn't been walking out of the Office to the bathroom when I thought I saw one of our housekeepers walking into the elevator alcove. Our elevator is ancient and very noisy. You can hear it even in the Office. I sped up to catch her and . . . Nobody was there! I described the housekeeper I had observed to one of the other Operators who had been there almost twenty-two years and she told me I had seen the ghost Edith!

That room had a number of very odd things happen in it while I worked there. One night I saw what appeared to be a fog in the Computer Room. Being concerned for the computers because of the strict need for control of humidity, I went in to see what had happened to the air conditioners . . . and the fog was gone. No fog on the windows.

Another night, I thought someone had broken into the Computer Room since I was hearing what sounded like barely audible voices. I could never learn where the sounds were coming from and even checked upstairs in ER to see if someone up there was screaming or something, but it was very quiet. That was very eerie. No one was outside, or in the halls. Edith never caused me any trouble and I was always on good terms with her.

HAUNTED HOUSE IN ENGLAND

Last winter, I lived for six weeks in a house in Rugby, England. It was a typical two-up, two-down house in fairly rough condition. I shared it with a colleague with whom I was working, who came from Ireland. He has told me that members of his family seem to be more perceptive than normal, and can 'sense' things such as emotional trauma in each other even if they are hundreds of miles apart. This could explain why he noticed such curious occurrences in the house while I, generally, did not.

Now and again, I would go home for the weekend leaving Jon alone in the house. He said that at night, he heard loud knocking and banging noises from downstairs, as if someone was slamming cupboard doors. One night he heard someone climbing the stairs and was convinced that it was a burglar. He got out of bed and hid in ambush at the top of the stairs, however, no-one appeared.

The central heating in the house was faulty, and we did not dare adjust its temperature in case it broke. Consequently, the house was maintained at a very high temperature, so much so that it was impossible to sleep under the bed covers in my bedroom. However, in Jon's room it was always bitterly cold, despite the presence of a large radiator which was too hot to touch. There were no drafts.

On one occasion, Jon was taking a bath. He heard the sound of something apparently scraping against the window pane and assumed again that it was a burglar. To his great surprise and fright, the bathroom mirror which was about two feet wide by five feet high and had been leaning against the wall on the other side of the room fell over and bounced off the floor making a huge crash but not breaking.

Toward the end of our occupancy, I was sitting

in the lounge reading at about 1:00 A.m., Jon having gone to bed about two hours previously. I suddenly felt very afraid, as if someone was watching me from the chair opposite. I could not stay in the room and hurried upstairs to my bed.

The next day, Jon (who was unaware of my experience of the night before) told me that he had awoke in the night and been aware of something white and shapeless at the end of his bed. He pulled the covers over his head and awoke the next morning still underneath them.

Throughout our time in the house, Jon had vivid and surreal dreams, including a very strange one about living in a coffin. It was, however, after we had left the house that he had a series of nightmares about the place, which started off with him being back in his bedroom at the house.

He would awaken to the sound of violent screaming from downstairs and open his door to see a man and a woman rush in a fit of panic up the stairs and into my bedroom. They were being pursued by a man-like figure with a purple cape, long flowing black hair and at least four arms, which he was using to haul himself up the narrow stairway.

As a final note, we met various other people from our company who had also visited the training college in Rugby. One of these people, totally unprompted, said something along the lines of 'I hated it there. I stayed in this house and every night there were crashing and banging sounds from downstairs. It was really frightening.' It turned out to be the same house as I had stayed in.

LIGHTHOUSE GHOST

This past summer I had the distinction of working as a gas attendant on third-shift. Because the town, Westerly, Rhode Island, is right on the shore, I had my share of fisherman who would come in every night for their ritual coffee before they hit the shores at 3:00 in the morning.

There were two gentlemen who had come down from Medford, Maine to do some shore casting, and being a native, they asked me for a good fishing spot that was nearby. I pointed them to the Watch Hill Light House, which has been standing in various incarnations for over one-hundred and fifty years. It was a favorite of other fishermen that frequented the station, so I did my good deed for the day and pointed them in the right direction.

The lighthouse itself is located on a peninsula that juts out about a mile from the shore, the lighthouse is surrounded by high walls and the road leading out to it is surrounded by wetland marsh. Although automated, the lighthouse still houses a keeper.

About an hour after I sent them on their way, the pair returned to the station, where upon one of the fishermen quickly made his way in and made a beeline for the rest room. His face was pale, causing me to gulp. I said to his friend, "He looks as though he saw a ghost." The mate chuckled and said, "He thinks he did."

At this point, I hear the other fellow in the bathroom spewing forth the junk he bought from the station just a few hours ago. After emerging, I questioned him about the incident . . .

In order to find the prime fishing hole, the two split up, when they reached the lighthouse. One went around one side while the other went the opposite way. They each were in the courtyard, within the walls, of the lighthouse, but were still separated from it by a chain-link fence.

One man's journey was uneventful. The other was going about the circumference of the lighthouse, shining his flashlight into the reeds at the bottom of the wall, which was about fifteen feet down, looking for a place to cast from.

As he went over one spot, he noted a mottled white bundle, possibly of cloth, and brought the light to the spot again to investigate. The mass shifted in the light and stood up, revealing a person of some sorts who stared up at him from the darkness and began shouting at him in some unintelligible language.

Concerned, but not overly frightened, the fisherman climbed the fence to go to the other side of the lighthouse to tell his friend that there was some homeless person or other denizen down below. He hoisted himself over the fence, and after getting over, turned back for a moment to find himself face to face with what was only a minute before was fifteen feet below him. This person or thing had climbed a fifteen-foot smooth concrete wall, silently.

He described her as a rotten old woman, with a foul-sea smell to her and black stumps in an oily black mouth. Her hair had assorted twigs in it and sea-refuse. He recoiled, as this woman shouted something garbled to him through the fence and as he shined the light on her face, noted that she did not have a tongue.

Obviously freaked, the fisherman bolted to the other side of the lighthouse to his friend, who had heard him scream but heard nothing else and presumed this whole thing to be a joke.

If you saw this man's face and he kept telling his story again and again, for over three hours. He really saw something.

I checked up on local folklore in my public library. In the Westerly Folklore section, the town records.

there is evidence that a woman was drowned off of the lighthouse peninsula by her husband around 1885, she was named Edith Whiting. Her husband allegedly cut her tongue out and killed her for having an affair while he was away at sea.

ATTACKED IN CANADA

First off, this is not something I enjoy telling people, because most of the time I get a good laugh and a 'sure, okay.' with a pat on the shoulder. Keeping that in mind . . .

I seem to have a little problem that has been snowballing for years now. When I was a kid, about age five, I started telling my parents that I could 'feel' stuff. They got a little worried, but it went away by about seven or eight. I said all sorts of weird stuff, like 'I can feel Bobb' and the like.

Most of this time, and quite often I guessed who was calling when the phone rang or who was at the door when the doorbell rang. I could guess which lottery ticket had a winner under the silver-stuff and so on to the point that my mother was seriously amused by me and showed me off at parties. I was pretty good at naming people's middle names, too.

Anyway, that's besides the point. The last thing I said at that age was a tale in and of itself. My mother found me, terrified, in my room, crying, screaming that 'Bobb is gone, Bobb is gone, he left me, he left me . . . ' and stuff.

About four years ago now, I moved to British Columbia. I have since returned, but the next part of this story happens there. I made a bunch of friends and was Mr. Normal teenager until, in one week, one friend overdosed on heroin.

I do not use drugs myself, never have, never will,

and was trying to help him kick the habit. Another friend fell off a cliff, and shattered his skull at the bottom. I found the bodies, both of them, got arrested for murder. I still think they were loony to think that I, this little skinny guy, could hold down a heroin addict long enough to pump him full of heroin against his will. The charges were dropped. At the time, it was my sixteenth birthday and my parents forgot all about it and weren't home.

So I had a complete emotional breakdown. I hope you find that understandable. I recovered rather quickly after about three months and have been fine ever since.

According to an 'expert' who has refused to allow me to use his name, I'm a little skeptical on this, I had to 'reboot', for lack of a better term, my entire mind. Then I accidentally, or purposefully, turned that stuff back on. Unfortunately, I've gotten a new aspect.

If 'Bobb' was ever my 'spirit protector', I really don't blame him for moving on. There's a new 'it' in my life, and the few times it has decided to name itself, it called itself 'R.E.B.'. I assume he is a male, from the glimpses and yes, I've seen it, and so have others who have been with me. I've caught, a Mennonite-ish hat and wire-rimmed glasses.

The little feelings, which I first called hunches, and later call flashes, started to happen more often over time. They were really small, and haven't gotten anywhere near to where I was when I was a kid. And they seem to work on physical closeness if they are bout people, instead of long-distance like it used to be.

I'll give an example, that didn't really make sense. I was walking in a mall, passed this average looking guy, and BAM, I know his name, his daughter's name. Plus, the fact that something bad is about to happen to her and he won't know until he gets to work tomorrow, which I think, by the way, was a cushy office job.

Now that happens, I'd say, about once or twice a month.

The flashes, which are a little less intense, happen more when I'm drunk so I don't drink, and are not as accurate. I get little flashes that now are a good time to buy a lottery ticket.

Or that maybe I should go to my room and change out of my best clothes and on the way to school I get blasted by mud somehow, and little annoying stuff like that. By the way I have won about eight hundred dollars this year by buying lottery tickets.

Then the other stuff started happening. First it was a glass. I'd go into my room, and pictures or mirrors had fallen, and almost always were broken. Glasses on the shelve in cupboards just had cracks in them when I opened the cupboards. A window cracked, A windscreen, A statuette and so on. When I started getting the feeling that there was someone nearby, then something broke.

Rarely a night goes by that I don't wake up because I feel like I'm being choked or scratched, and I wake up with bruises or scratches. These cannot be self inflicted, as they are sometimes in places I could never reach because of the angle or position.

I try not to drink out of glass cups because they tend to shatter. I've got more little scars on my hands than I can relate, and occasionally, I've opened the cupboard and find crushed glass.

Then it started happening to my closest friends, when I was around. I was at home with three people playing a card game. The phone rang, and I answered it and it was my friend from Fisherville.

Anyway, suddenly, all of the cupboards in the kitchen blast open. Outside doors first, moving in to the center. I'm on the phone, and the cupboards blew open, then, and my three friends hear this voice that says "Thirsty?"

The girl on the telephone said, "Did someone say

my name?" Her name is Kristin.

Then, one after the other, glasses pitched themselves at me. I decided that dropping the phone would be good, followed by running away. Meanwhile, glass is shattering everywhere. So I turn to leave and I feel a wind behind me. I look, stopping, since the glasses just stopped, and I get my 'feeling' that I know it is R.E.B.

The best way I can describe it was that he was 'pulling himself together', as if there were pieces of him all over that he had to gather to make what he did work. I saw his hat, his glasses, and a piece of his nose. My friends, who were beside me now, in the family room entrance arch, were agape.

Then R.E.B. finished pulling himself together, this took maybe three seconds, and I moved up and back. I would say I got punched, and I sort of hopped 'up' into the air first, then back and down the stairs I went. I had a bruise on my stomach from where the blast hit for almost four days.

THE BARKING DOG

Just wanted to relate an experience that is happening right now in our house. Several months ago my wife brought home a large round picture from a yard sale. It is old, over forty years or so, but not ancient.

It has a round wooden frame painted gold. The picture itself is a reproduction of a Victorian type image of two young girls, one about ten, and the other about four years of age. They are smiling and talking together. The entire picture is about 2.5 feet in diameter. It's been hanging in our hallway ever since.

About four months ago, we got a new dog, a puppy who is growing up fast. Now that she has the run of the house, she's started to explore. Last week, she suddenly seemed to notice the painting and started barking at it.

At first she was pretty mellow about it, but now, almost every other day she starts an intense barking session, standing directly under the painting and staring at it. It's very strange, but we get her to stop, and it does not bother her again until the next episode.

UNIVERSITY OF TORONTO GHOST

If you are ever in Toronto, Canada, visit Hart House at the downtown campus of University of Toronto. Apparently, the story goes, at the turn of the century when the building was being built, two Russian immigrants were hired to help in building the gargoyles that line the top of the building.

Both men fell in love with a young woman in town and competed for her. It got to a point where one, in a jealous rage, attacked the other with an axe on the roof of the building. He took a swing with the axe, missed and fell over the side of the Hart House and died.

Fearing the authorities, the others buried the body somewhere on the site and during a fire a few years later, investigators found skeletal remains. Now if you go to the roof of the building, on one of the doors there should still be axe marks from the attack. Then two of the gargoyles that the two men were working on, one seems to be laughing behind the other's back.

The ghost story is that years later, on a cold winter's day, a student was walking down the basement halls of Hart House and chanced upon a man sitting at a table drinking vodka. The man offered the student a drink and said, "cold day isn't it?" When the student turned to reply, the man disappeared!

GHOSTS IN MEXICO

I studied at the Universaidad de las Americas (University of the Americas) in Puebla Mexico. The site where the campus is located used to be a deserted hacienda. Along the periphery of the campus are a very old graveyard and a deserted convent where four nuns and a priest were killed a long time ago.

Many people have claimed to see a figure of a woman standing in the top window of the convent. There are many rumors of the existence of a ghost on the campus. This story took place in the dorm.

There are three dorms on the campus. Two are women's dorms and one is the men's dorm. The dorms are separated into ten, three-story buildings lettered from 'A to J'. The ghost is said to be located on the third floor in building 'A' in the suite the Resident Assistants (RA) lives.

Obviously, no one wants to be a RA in that building, so they draw straw to see who gets it. One summer, my friend had to be the RA for building A. He told me how he and a friend (another RA) saw a paper weight and a pen float through the air. (Both told me the same story on separate occasions); But this is not the story.

This is the story. One Saturday afternoon, my friend was lying on his bed in his room while listening to his Walkman radio, the lights were out and the door was closed. He was feeling relaxed until he saw someone's feet at the bottom of the door. He went to see who it was, but no one was there. He went back to his bed to listen to his music and out of the corner of his eye he saw a apparition or figure floating toward him and away from him repeatedly.

He turned on the lights and the figure disappeared. He thought he was seeing things, so he just turned the lights off and again the figure did the same thing. Again he turned off the lights and the figure disappeared.

He waited for a few minutes and turned the lights off and, again, he saw the figure so he pulled his blanket over his head all of a sudden he heard breathing in his ear. It was not until this point that he decided to run out of the room, but something held him down. He tried for a long time to get up until he tired out and fell asleep. When he awoke, he found bruises all over his body.

When he finished his story, I told him that there was no way that I would believe him. But in the years that I've known him, he has never lied to me and he had a very serious look on his face when he told me. I can't help believing him. I have a lot of friends in Mecicom and other parts of Latin America who has claimed to have an experience with a ghost.

I lived on the first floor of the same building a year later. Every Sunday I sat at my desk to do homework. I always left the door open to let the air circulate. At around three o'clock every Sunday I always saw an apparition or figure walking into the bathroom. I lived with seven other people in the suite. It was common for one of us to say 'hi' when someone walked in. I went into the bathroom to see who it was and no one was there!

THE BLACK CAT

In April of 1985, I have had some kind of experience and I am not sure what it was. I was in my bedroom during a storm. I remember that it was not a big storm. I remember that I was sitting on my bed when suddenly, I heard what sounded like a herd of cattle stomping through the house.

There was no one else in the house except me, with the exception of a black cat who was out in the living room sitting on the back of a chair. I got really scared from hearing the strange sounds coming from outside my bedroom.

I slowly opened the bedroom door and cautiously looked down the hallway but I could not see anything nor did I hear anything else. I finally got enough courage to leave the bedroom so I walked out to living room to investigate what had made so much noise.

There was nothing in the living room except my black cat sleeping on the back of the chair. The noise had not disturbed the black cat I heard in the bedroom. I still to this day have no idea what could have made all that noise for it truly sounded like a herd of cattle stomping through the house.

THE CROOKED PICTURE

There is another story about that house that I would like to relate. The house belonged to my former sister-in-law. She was a fanatic concerning pictures on her wall. Every time anybody would straighten the pictures on the wall after she passed away, strange things happened. If you straighten a picture and then turned your back and immediately looked back to the picture, then that picture would be crooked again.

The night I was going to get married, we went

through the house straightening every picture on the wall so they all would look even. We would turn our back and then look back at the picture. The straightened pictures would be hung crooked on the wall!

Whenever, we looked at the pictures, they would remain straight but when we turned our backs on the pictures and turned back, then the straightened pictures would be hung crooked on the wall again! We don't know why or how it would occur except my ex-sister-in-law hated straight pictures.

THE WALKING MIRROR

Another time, while we were living in that house, we had a great big mirror mounted on top of the fireplace mantel. One night the big mirror jumped off the fireplace mantel and walked over to the dining area next to a dish hutch. We still do not understand how something like this could have happened since that large mirror is extremely heavy and takes two people to move it.

These two incidences happened while we were living in Euless, Texas. My ex-sister-in-law who was the owner of the house, had died in the house. We felt it was her keeping the things in the house just the way it was when she was alive.

FOOTSTEPS IN THE NIGHT

I had another incident when I was a young girl and went on a vacation with my mother and father traveling through Colorado. Back in those days' one could rent a house by the night just like one can do at a motel.

My mother and father rented a two-story house

for one night. My sister and I were in one bedroom and my parents were in the other bedroom at the far end of the house.   There was a bedroom in the middle between our bedroom and our parents.   My parents wanted us in the far bedroom so we would not keep them awake with our talking.

While we were laying in bed talking, we heard someone walk out of the vacant middle bedroom. It sounded like a woman who was wearing a long dress because it made a swishing sound as she walked down the stairs. We didn't get up out of bed to go look because I was somewhat frightened. We heard her walk down the stairs then through the hallway into the kitchen. We heard the faucet turn on and then turn off and then the swishing sound like being made by a long dress dragging on the floor as she walked back up the stairs and went into the middle bedroom. We don't know that it was a woman but we just suspected so.

GOD OR THE DEVIL

The following story comes from St. Helens Oregon but occurred while she was living in Imperial Beach, California. There was a slough behind the house. The slough was once used as part of the salt mine. An old railroad track runs down along the slough and the local children will go down there to play.

One Sunday night, my son comes home with this devil's head. The head was the size of a normal human head and he told me he had found it in the slough. I went next door and got my girlfriend Terry to come over. The head was really ugly and we were making jokes about it, thinking nothing of it really. The head had been found partially buried down in the slough.

I found out later that the head, carved out of lava, was very porous. It was hand carved and it had what I would call horns or long ears. It had a slash and then like teardrops coming down the eye and it would not stand upright. The head looked like it had been part of a statue at one time, and was maybe knocked off.

I had the head in the house and later that day

Terry came over and asked to borrow the head to show some friends. She took the head and put it into her garage. She went out that evening and had a babysitter attend her children. Later that evening, I got a call from her babysitter saying she had seen a strange man in her front yard.

I went into my garage so I could get a better look at whom was standing in my friend's yard. I saw a tall thin man, all in black wearing a hat, standing in Terry's front yard. The yard has a locked gate that surrounds the yard. The strange man was standing inside the yard and locked gate. This strange man was standing in the middle of my neighbor's yard on her walkway.

The babysitter said she had tried to call the police but their telephone was busy. I went into my home and tried to call the police, but I too found their line busy. Later when I did get through to the police, they said all six lines had been open all evening and there was no way a busy signal was possible. Now you must understand that Imperial Beach is about the size of St. Helens and has very few problems in the evenings.

In the next couple of days, little things began happening that started to worry us. I had the head back at my house by this time. That night, my husband and I were in bed when I suddenly awakened from sleep very cold. My back was facing my husband. I felt like I was being stared at. I turned over to look at my husband. He was staring at me with a really ugly and threatening look on his face, like he was ready to strike me. I shook him, he closed his eyes and returned to sleep. In asking him about it the next morning, he had no memory of it.

According to Gary Shaw, Star News Staff Writer who wrote an article that said, in part, " . . . her kids were scared and the babysitter was shaking. They'd seen someone or something, all black, tall and scraggly, drifting outside the window."

"When the light hits it at night, it sparkles . . .
Looking at his face, he has a slash through the eyeball.
Slashes on the neck. Tears drop under the right eye .
. . It has horns or pointed ears, widespread nostrils,
the most evil expression and cat-shaped slanted eyes."

"We've taken it to different museums and they
don't want it around. They're afraid to have it around
. . . The guy from the Museum of Man said it was from
central Mexico."

GRANDMOTHER'S HOUSE

My grandmother's house is old and in the coun-
try. They bought this house after their first one burned
down. In one of the upstairs bedrooms they have nick-
named one room "the ghost room." One day I asked
what this meant and I found out some interesting
things. One night my aunt (four or five years of age)
was sleeping in this room and she awoke to find a man
standing at the foot of her bed staring at her. She
freaked and would never sleep in there again. Another
night, my mother was sleeping in there when she awoke
to hear someone sleeping beside her. She felt the other
side of the bed but there was no one there. But instead of freaking, she just went back to sleep.

THE FALLING PICTURE

I have a really cool story about a picture that
kept falling down. You can make of it what you like,
but my family will always believe she was doing it. My
Dad was very close to his father's mother. She adored
him when he was growing up and just loved him to
pieces. She was his advocate for everything. Unfortunately, she died while he was away in the service.

Later, after my Mom and Dad got married, my mom cross-stitched a nice scene for my Grandparents. They loved it and decided to hang it up on the wall. They took down a picture of my Dad when he was just a child and hung the picture my Mom made in its place. A few hours later, we were all sitting around when we heard a thump. We found the picture they'd just hung was on the floor. It was put back up. But again, it fell! Then, a third time it fell to the floor. Now the picture that had been up of my Dad had been there for many years and had never fallen.

My Grandparents tried everything to make it stay up on the wall. But no matter what, the picture would fall. Finally, in jest, my Grandmother said that it must be my great-grandmother who kept knocking the picture down. So we decide to test this out. We hung my Dad's picture back up on the wall. Guess what--it is still there and hasn't fallen yet!

THE SPOTLIGHT

I thought I'd share our family "ghost" with you all. When I was five years old, my grandfather got very ill with cancer. My parents decided to make a 'hospital room' for him in our den. Within a few months of moving into the 'hospital room', my grandfather died of the cancer. My grandfather was an artist. He had painted a beautiful seaside painting for my parents which they hung in the dining room. The picture was set-off by a spotlight.

On the birthday of my grandfather, the year after his death, the spotlight went out. Then, on the anniversary of his death, the spotlight goes out! Then for over nineteen years, the light bulb or spotlight over the beautiful seaside painting goes out on the birthday of my grandfather and on the anniversary of his death.

When I was young, it spooked me but now that I am no longer living with my parents, it is nice to know that my grandfather is still "around" and putting in his two-cents worth, at least twice a year.

RAISED WITH A POLTERGEIST

Yes, I have had a few experiences. I grew up with a Poltergeist in my home as a child that favored me over my sisters. I witnessed a couple apparitions and ringing doorbells with nobody there. I could hear the ring and had a clear shot of the door bell. I also witnessed the slamming of cupboards, the hiding of personal property, scrawling on my clothes overnight, knocking on walls and bumping of my bed at night.

When I tried to trade rooms with my nonbeliever and younger sister, her hair was pulled while she was in my old room, and the bumping of her bed. She returned to her room and I slept on the floor for a while till my parents said it wouldn't hurt me.

Later, I lived in a house with my husband, before we married. Every time he tried to touch me, the walls would bang loudly and wake up our house guests. The two house guests decided that it had to be the plumbing pipe in the wall. They went under the house and found no pipes at all at that end of the house.

Another time, the floor would squeak as if someone was pacing the floor. My two house guests wouldn't go to sleep without the lights on! We moved after that.

HAUNTED BARRACKS

Here is a true story that I would like to share. My father told it to me. About twenty-five years ago my dad was serving in the Peace Corps. He was a well-digger stationed in Bophal, India, but he also traveled around to various villages.

There was an abandoned barracks which was supposedly haunted. Many soldiers had died there of malaria. My dad was skeptical, so his buddies dared him to sleep there. Naturally he accepted the dare.

One night he and his buddies went there. My dad went inside while his friends stayed outside. My dad laid down in one of the bunks and just as he was about to fall asleep he was picked up and thrown out of the bunk.

He thought that it was one of his pals so he said "Which one of you jokers was that?" There was no response. He went outside where his friends were waiting and said "Who threw me out of the bunk?"

They all denied it. So, he went back inside and barricaded the door so that no one could get in to play a prank on him. When he laid down he was picked up and thrown out of the bunk again. But there was no one there! No one living at any rate. He hightailed it out of there and never returned.

A PERSONAL GHOST STORY

I go to college at the University of Michigan. Last fall a few of my friends moved into a house off campus. It began to become apparent that the house was haunted.

I thought, "Yeah, right."

After a while though the evidence began to wear away at even my skepticism. My friends got out an Ouija board and found out that the ghost was a four-year-old boy named Tyler. I didn't buy it. Then my friend's three-year old daughter stared, pointing to blank walls and saying, "Who's that?"

The neighbor's cat which would sleep in the house

would sometimes become extremely hyper. (I know all cats do) But this cat, a Siamese, would chase what seemed to be nothing all over the house. Literally, she would go from a dead sleep to an instant explosion of energy.

Now Tyler obviously was not a malicious ghost but he was rather naughty. The thing that finally convinced me was his habit of hiding important things, most notably the car keys. One evening my friend hung his keys on the peg over the kitchen sink. An hour later our other friend called for us to pick him up. We searched for the keys for an hour! We found them the next day in a match box in the furnace room next to the water heater.

Tyler was just playing games, but he could be affected. For example, whenever we would lose something, my friend's mother would get angry and say she was going to move out, invariably what we looked for would turn up in the next few minutes.

THE NATURE OF GHOSTS

There are three prevailing ideas that suggest the nature of ghosts that haunt this plane of existence. Unfortunately, there is no absolute proof for any of these ideas. However, empirical evidence and application of old fashion gray cells' often reveal interesting correlations that support at least one of these elementary hypotheses.

The first idea considers that ghosts are emotion fragments, echoes of a powerful emotion that float about as a ripple in the magnetic field of the place they occupied. It is suggested that certain houses tend to adopt, amplify and elicit certain moods stemming from a painful event.

The second idea considers that ghosts could be soul fragments, bits of people lost in painful events and doomed to wander aimlessly through this physical domain. It would be a frightening thought to believe that our souls could become fragmented at the time of death. This fragmented soul would roam the land due to painful events within our lives.

The authors subscribe to the third and perhaps more interesting hypotheses concerning the nature of ghosts. The idea of ectoplasmic transformation as the basic explanation for ghosts. This idea is not new, but is a part of most parapsychological interpretation currently expressed in paranormal investigations.

When a person departs this life, his mortal body decays into the basic elements or original particles of the earth. When the life force of an individual surrender's to death, the life force is transformed back into its basic electromagnetic energy components. This idea is like down loading a program from your hard drive to a floppy disk. The program is saved but on a different media. This energy field retains the intelligence of its former mortal life while existing in its new state.

At the time of death measurements of this electromagnetic field or EMF energy field is detectable. This reading on an EMF meter would denote a significant increase in electromagnetic energy flow across the terminals of the meter.

The life force or energy survives death. This life force or energy cannot be destroyed. The new EMF energy must conform to the laws of thermal-dynamics. The life force that now exists in the corresponding but different energy patterns are what we would now know as spirit energy.

The intelligence of the individual that existed previously continues in its new paradigm. This intelligent entity must discover and use the Access Port or Energy Gates to progress beyond this plane of physical existence.

These Energy Gates or Access Ports described by some individuals, who have departed this life and could return to this mortal life, as 'tunnels of lights'. The pathway allows these spirit entities to bridge the gap from this plane of physcial existence, to their new realm. This realm lies somewhere beyond our time and space.

Since not all people who pass into death are happy and content, there are those individuals who at the time of death have emotions filled with hate and anger or are in a state of confusion. Immediately upon their death, these confused or malcontent spirits may choose not to continue through the 'tunnel of lights' but feels more content to remain behind in this plane.

There may be many reasons why a spirit may choose not to use the 'tunnel of light' and continue to the realm of other spirit entities. Just because a spirit does not enter this 'tunnel of light' does not mean that it is evil or corrupt. As in life, one has to make many decisions, whose outcome will affect one's life, so too in death.

More often then not, the spirit entities that will attach or align themselves with people of like mindedness. A positive spirit may match up with positive behavior patterns and negative spirits may search out negative behavior. Confused or malcontent spirit entities feed on negative energy that abounds in the lives of angry and unstable people. These people are not evil but unfortunately their disposition is toward negativism. They shall remain in this plane of existence until they can resolve the emotional linkage. There is no set period for this. It is entirely dependent upon the spirit entity and their ability to resolve the problems holding them back.

Then there are those spirit entities who chose to come back from time to time to oversee the affairs of their loved ones. This overriding emotion of love is strong, even at death. Perhaps, these are the entities which become either the guardian angels or the loved ones who help us in our times of crisis?

When the affairs of the spirit entities are in order or the unresolved emotional issues resolved, then the compelling reasons for the spirit entities remaining in this plane of existence are no longer dominant and the spirit entities pass over to the other side.

Perhaps some spirit entities have analogous and compelling emotional ties to this plane of existence and are not willing to let go to them. Thus, they will haunt a place that has deep emotional affinity to their mortal life. This can often be their old home where they have died.

Sometimes a confused spirit entity will roam the land not believing they are dead. They become more angry over time because of their confused state. This anger is expressed as rage and directed toward those living on this plane of existence. These confused and restless spirits do not know how to depart from this plane or lack understanding on how to depart. These spirits become restless and often malevolence, express- ing their anger in the only way they know how.

Sometimes a child will die and become confused about where he or she is at. The frightened deceased child wants their mother to help. This state of confu- sion may very well prevent the child from crossing over to the other side. The child will roam the land, playing pranks on people, while looking for their loved ones.

These pranks will continue until such a time as the child can come to terms with whom they are and what they must do to find the bliss they are seeking. For whatever reason, entities use their pranks and ac- tivity as a means of getting our attention.

The time schedule of this awakening is accord- ing to the progress of the child and not according to the progress of a priest performing a exorcism ritual. No disrespect is intended to men of the cloth who be- lieve that religious rituals will banish ghostly entities from this mortal realm. Unfortunately, this type of ritual is not effective unless the ghostly entity has al- ready decided to depart prior to the exorcism.

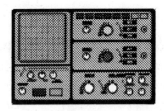

DETECTION OF GHOSTS

The arrival of solid state electronics began the era of high technology. Today, hi-tech electronic equipment has made it possible to be able to now detect and monitor the presence of spirit entities. Science has come a long way since the turn of the century in paranormal research.

Popular programs such as Unsolved Mysteries and Sightings have had ghost hunters walking around with electronic gear searching for ghostly entities. The electronic gear used by these ghost hunters is not top secret or developed by covert government operations for the elite.

We shall describe the equipment and where this electronic equipment can be purchased. Based on our experiences while writing this book, there are three general methods for detecting the supernatural forces which we are calling ghosts. Ghost hunting can be fun and exciting for anyone.

The cost to purchase the various equipment is low compared to other hobbies and the benefits are unbelievable. Consider the benefit of knowledge gained concerning the afterlife. Ghosts are people whose physical bodies have died, yet their spirits remain on this life plane to haunt.

EMF FIELD METHOD

The first method uses the Electromagnetic Field Detector which scans for electromagnetic fields from thirty hertz to four hundred hertz. This Detector is available at most electronic supply houses. There are several basic EMF models on the market which will function very well in ghost hunting.

The authors are using the portable electromagnetic field tester, produced by A.W. Sperry Instruments, Inc., model EMF-200A, with an EMF range of zero to 199.9 milligauss and a large LCD display. Model EMF-200A operates on a standard nine-volt battery and is small enough to fit inside your shirt pocket. It may lack some more sophisticated circuitry of larger and more expensive units with bells and whistles but it is sufficient to detect the various shifts in the electromagnetic fields. It is not the cost of the equipment but its function that is important.

EMF field detectors have one purpose, register the signal strength of the electromagnetic fields within the frequency range the unit was designed for. The EMF detector monitors any changes in the background EMF radiation levels.

THERMOMETER METHOD

The second method involves the measurement of the temperatures which will reveal 'cold spots' which seem to move about within a room. These 'cold spots' are the cold air felt on the back of the neck, or the coldness felt within a supposedly haunted room. This physical change in temperature is a result of the spirit energy fields generated by the entities.

This piece of equipment is the digital readout thermometer produced by Tandy Corporation, Radio

Shack catalog number 63-844. Micronta is the brand name of this unit. This unit has the combination LCD twin display for the thermometer and the hygrometer. This unit records the temperature changes in tenths of a degree which is sufficient for ghost hunting.

The thermometer becomes another tool to record the movement of supernatural entities by monitoring the change in the temperature. We do not understand why the temperature is affected but it is sufficient to know that there is a correlation. The explanation may have to be provided at a later date as more knowledge is gained by other ghost hunters.

PHOTOGRAPHY METHOD

The third method is ghost photography. It relies on the fact that the energy field surrounding the ghost or that the composition of the ghost is in the infrared range and can be photographed by using infrared film with an 87c filter or red filter on the camera. This spirit entity or energy field may be captured on infrared film or on Polaroid film.

Polaroid is a transparent material containing embedded crystals capable of polarizing light. Perhaps this polarization of light allows the spirit entities to become visible. Whatever the reason, Polaroid film has been used successfully in recording ghostly images on film. It is perhaps the least expensive route to follow in ghost photography since the developing is done instantly and the results can be viewed immediately.

It is interesting that if one considers that small children and some animals can see in the infrared range or polarized light, it is not surprising that these children may be the one's that may really see ghosts and not be talking to imaginery characters.

APPLICATION

Now let us consider how we would apply the three tools to detect ghosts. We would start off with the EMF tester. The normal background radiation level is ususally below .8 mG with an average reading of .2 to .5 mG.

Therefore, if readings are obtained in the 1.3mG or 1.4mG range or larger and the signal remain steady at the higher reading, then a target has been acquired. If excessive readings are obtained, be sure to check for an external source of EMF that is generating the excessive readings. Once we have obtained a higher then normal reading on the EMF tester, scan with the digital thermometer for a drop in temperature.

Use the digital readout temperature meter to record temperatures from around the room. If the temperature meter detects a cool or cold spot, then reconfirm with the EMF tester for a distribution in the electromagnetic field. Should both be present, photographing the area with infrared film or with a Polaroid camera should yield interesting results.

Just because we do not understand the physical principle operating for a given paranormal event does not mean a physical principle is not in operation. It is important to keep an open mind while investigating ghostly events.

GHOST PHOTOGRAPHY

In the beginning of our venture to gather supernatural occurrences for our book, my mind pondered
the possibility of photographing spirits. Ghost Photography, I was certain would require some complex,
expensive, high-tech gadgets to accomplish such a task.
As we looked into the experience of others involved in
paranormal investigating, we discovered we were quite
wrong!

Some of the best photographs taken, displaying
a spirit entity, have been on film as simple as Polaroid
film. Polaroid film develops in sixty seconds. The special developing process and the chemical makeup of
the film allow it to be more likely to pick up a ghostly
form. Also, by its developing on the spot, the picture is
more credible than other films. It is almost impossible
to double-expose Polaroid film, for creating an extra
image that is not there.

We started using the Polaroid Captiva Camera
with 95 Captiva film. It is light weight, compact and
easy to use in situations where I need a camera, ready
to go in a hurry. I also use a 35-mm camera for the
high speed Black & White and a 35-mm camera for the
infrared shooting.

If we want to photograph these ghostly apparitions then there are three general ways that have proven

successful in the past.

We have mentioned that the spirit entities operate in the infrared range of visible light. Accordingly, the first method for photographing ghostly apparitions is by using high speed Black & White Infrared film with a 35-mm camera that can shoot in the infrared range.

This is the best method for recording onto photographic film, the ghostly apparitions of spirit entities. Infrared film is sensitive to light, so the loading and unloading of this film has to be accomplished in total darkness. The infrared film, sealed in a protective canister, must be opened in the dark.

The second method of photographing ghostly images is by using a Polaroid camera using instant film such as 600 instant films or the new Captiva 95 instant film. It seems that the Polaroid film may be more receptive to energy disturbances in the infrared range then the more conventional 35-mm film.

The third method of photographing ghostly images is by using very fast 35-mm film, with speeds from 1,600 or 3,200. Kodak offers a high speed film rated at ASA 3,200. Fuji offers their NeoPan with ASA rated at 1,600.

The authors have seen photographs that depict areas of high energy motion on 35-mm, color, ASA 400 films. Several photographs, given to the authors, taken with a regular point-and-shoot camera using a low speed film of ASA 100, shooting indoors with a flash.

These photographs contained an energy field

surrounding an individual. Most of the time, no ghostly apparition will appear unless there is a strong electromagnetic field that will 'boot' the energy fields of the spirit into more visible ranges detected by normal film.

There are no boundaries on what equipment or films are best as it seems it is more a matter of shooting in the right place at the right time. Videotaping is another excellent manner in which to film as you can take in more area with film rolling than shooting frame by frame still shots. Good luck and good hunting!

INDEX

intelligence 163

J

Jester, Heather 86
Johnson, Chris 87

K

Kelley, Leslie 47, 49, 52, 53
Kennedy, Kathy 19, 20, 91
KEX 95
keys 77, 78, 83, 87, 161
Knight Hall 93, 94
Knowles, Joseph 46
Kosharek, Pat 95

L

Lessard, Jeri 85
Lewis and Clark 44, 66
Liberty Theater 20, 45, 46, 47, 50, 52, 53
light bulb 70, 158
Lily 49
Little Jack Richie 46
Lombardo, Guy 46

M

Maori wars 134
Mary 50, 51, 52
McMaster, Elena 53
mirror 51, 141, 153
music 68, 74, 81, 82, 84, 86, 92
music box 69

N

NBC Evening Magazine 20
NBC Good Evening 20
noise 47, 58, 68, 75, 76, 81, 106, 108, 137, 152
noises 111

O

Oester, Carolina 107
Oester, Sarah 112

THE AUTHORS

Dave R. Oester, age 47, started writing his first adventure horror novel shortly after moving to the coastal town of Seaside, Oregon. Oester's background is filled with the adventure and excitement that he writes about. His background includes the following: Boy Scout Adult Leader, Insurance Agent, Accountant in Public Practice, Comptroller, Business Consultant, Oil & Gas Driller, Geophysical Consultant, Inventor, Paralegal Technician, Professional Treasure Hunter, Paranormal Investigator and Writer. Oester is currently researching material for two new books. The first book is ghosts tales, volume two. The second book will be dealing with the Petroglyphs of Early Man in the Lava Beds National Monument. Oester has done extensive research on the interpretation of petroglyphs of the Southwest.

Sharon A. Gill, age 45, started her formal writing career with this book and is currently researching new material for the next series of books dealing with unseen visitors from beyond the grave. She is currently photographing petroglyphs for their book on Petroglyph of Early Man in the Lava Beds National Monument. She has had a colorful background in such professions as Nursing, Paralegal Technician, Outdoor & Wildlife Photographer and Writer. She enjoys traveling, researching ghost stories and old ghost towns of the western United States. Gill enjoys paranormal investigation combined with photography. She does her own darkroom work for color and black & white prints. Gill is a graduate of New York Institute of Photography.

To order additional copies of **Twilight Visitors: Gh**
complete the information below.

Ship to: (please print)

Name _____

Address _____

City, State, Zip _____

Day phone _____

_____ copies of *Twilight Visitors...* @ $13.95 each $_____

Postage and handling @ $2.50 per book $ _____

Total amount enclosed $ _____

*Make checks payable to **Starwest Images***

**Send to: Starwest Images
P.O. Box 976 • St. Helens, OR 97051
(503) 397-0686**

- -

To order additional copies of **Twilight Visitors: Ghost Tales!**,
complete the information below.

Ship to: (please print)

Name _____

Address _____

City, State, Zip _____

Day phone _____

_____ copies of *Twilight Visitors...* @ $13.95 each $_____

Postage and handling @ $2.50 per book $ _____

Total amount enclosed $ _____

*Make checks payable to **Starwest Images***

**Send to: Starwest Images
P.O. Box 976 • St. Helens, OR 97051
(503) 397-0686**